# Who put the {DEVIL} in DEVILED EGGS?

# Who put the {DEVIL} in DEVILED EGGS?

THE FASCINATING STORIES BEHIND AMERICA'S
FAVORITE FOODS

## ANN TREISTMAN

To LeAnna Weller Smith, the best designer in the world!
With thanks to Meg Distinti and Kristin Kulsavage.

Skyhorse Publishing books may be purchased in bulk at special discounts for
sales promotion, corporate gifts, fund-raising, or educational purposes. Special
editions can also be created to specifications. For details, contact the Special Sales
Department, Skyhorse Publishing, 307 West 36th Street,
11th Floor, New York, NY 10018 or info@skyhorsepublishing.com.

www.skyhorsepublishing.com

10 9 8 7 6 5 4 3 2

Library of Congress Cataloging-in-Publication Data is available on file.
ISBN: 978-1-60239-742-2

Printed in China

TELL ME WHAT YOU EAT AND
I WILL TELL YOU WHAT YOU ARE.

—Jean Anthelme Brillat-Savarin,
*The Physiology of Taste* (1825)

~~

THE MOST REMARKABLE THING ABOUT MY
MOTHER IS THAT FOR THIRTY YEARS SHE SERVED
THE FAMILY NOTHING BUT LEFTOVERS.

THE ORIGINAL MEAL HAS NEVER BEEN FOUND.

—Calvin Trillin

# contents

*Who put the* [DEVIL] *in* DEVILED EGGS?

# INTRODUCTION

IN THE HOPE THAT HER SYSTEM OF COOKERY MAY BE CONSULTED WITH EQUAL ADVANTAGE BY FAMILIES IN TOWN AND IN COUNTRY, BY THOSE WHOSE CONDITION MAKES IT EXPEDIENT TO PRACTISE ECONOMY, AND BY OTHERS WHOSE CIRCUMSTANCES AUTHORIZE A LIBERAL EXPENDITURE, THE AUTHOR SENDS IT TO TAKE ITS CHANCE AMONG THE MULTITUDE OF SIMILAR PUBLICATIONS, SATISFIED THAT IT WILL MEET WITH AS MUCH SUCCESS AS IT MAY BE FOUND TO DESERVE, MORE SHE HAS NO RIGHT TO EXPECT.

—Eliza Leslie, *Directions for Cookery, in its Various Branches* (1840)

**WHY DEVILED EGGS** and not stuffed mushrooms? Why apple and pumpkin pies, and not peach or blueberry? What *is* this eclectic mix of dishes—some of which might only be eaten in one region of the nation and scorned in another? Needless to say, it is rather a mash-up of various foods, but in a way—how appropriate.

Thinking about American cookery from its very roots reveals how nearly everything we eat came from Europe with settlers. It also makes very clear the elaborate—and sometimes random—updates and changes that have been made to these dishes.

Brownies were once prepared without chocolate (is a brownie without chocolate really a brownie, you might ask?). Pumpkin pie was made with rosemary, thyme, and apples. Granula, a precursor to today's granola, was hard as a rock, and had to be soaked in milk before it was eaten. Biscuits went from twice-cooked pucks taken on ship journeys because they never became stale (they started out that way), to the flaky, buttery mounds we enjoy today. Peanuts for peanut butter were once boiled, not roasted. And there are dozens of variations on meatloaf; we added the ketchup and the cheese.

About the recipes themselves: I've included many simple ones from the late 1800s and early 1900s. These may have been handed down from early European immigrants or even from ancient Rome, but those printed here represent the first ones published in America. It's fascinating to see how little emphasis was placed on measurements.

Perhaps these old recipes will inspire you to pick half a dozen apples, cut them up, and toss in some sugar to make a pie, without having to roll the dough exactly right or worry about how much liquid will seep from the crust, and so forth. It's quite wonderful to see the words of our past and find a connection with the present through these recipes.

I hope you will enjoy the roundabout journey. Let me know if there's something that absolutely needs to be included next time around!

Ann Treistman
New York City

# MACARONI AND CHEESE

IF YOU DON'T LIKE MACARONI AND CHEESE, YOU DON'T
KNOW HOW TO HAVE A GOOD TIME.

—Ina Garten, The Barefoot Contessa

**MACARONI AND CHEESE** is the easiest comfort food you'll ever make. Hot pasta tossed with cheese and butter at its base, the combination appeals to children and adults alike. Yet for such a simple recipe, it's hard to pinpoint exactly where this dish was first created.

Oh, mysterious macaroni. Historians and archaeologists have yet to answer the question: Who invented pasta? The two major theories claim that fresh noodles were first crafted either by ancient Etruscans in Italy or by peasants in ancient China. Other evidence suggests that dried noodles were being sold and consumed by Arab peoples as early as the 5th century CE.

Pasta had made its way north through Europe sometime after the 15th century, when the art of drying noodles was perfected in Italy. Americans were slow to warm to the dish, but the English of the industrial age quickly embraced the time-saving staple. Historical rumor states that macaroni first migrated to the United States when Thomas Jefferson returned from France with the first pasta makers in 1789.

Mary Randolph, a cookbook writer close to Jefferson's family, published an early recipe for macaroni and cheese in her cookbook *The Virginia Housewife* in 1838. This early support by Jefferson and his family might explain why homemade macaroni and cheese has become a Southern "soul food" specialty in the United States.

## THE DEVIL'S IN THE DETAILS

There are entire cookbooks devoted to macaroni and cheese. Additions to the genre include shaved truffles, bacon, buttered bread crumbs, diced ham, broccoli, peas, lobster, caramelized onions, pesto, and every kid's favorite addition: hot dogs!

In 1918, another discovery made traditional American macaroni and cheese even easier to make: Velveeta. This "cheese product" was created by a Swiss immigrant named Emil Frey, for the Monroe Cheese Company in Monroe, New York. What makes this different from regular cheese, is how the whey and curd are bound together so they don't separate at all when heated. This makes for a pretty creamy mac and cheese. Perhaps that's why the Velveeta Cheese Company was made its own company in 1923, and then sold to Kraft Foods in 1927.

Outside the South, macaroni and cheese may be thought of as more blue than yellow. In 1937, the Kraft Cheese Company introduced the first boxed version of macaroni and cheese in blue-and-yellow packaging with the slogan, "A meal for 4 . . . in 9 minutes." The timing was perfect. Not only was the boxed dinner a hit on its own, but when World War II ignited just a few years later, Kraft became a great resource for riveting Rosies who were expected to cook after a full day of work.

# MACARONI I, AS USUALLY SERVED WITH THE CHEESE COURSE

from *The Book of Household Management* by Isabella Mary Beeton (1861)

1/2 pound of pipe macaroni

1/4 pound of butter

6 ounces of Parmesan or Cheshire cheese

pepper and salt to taste

1 pint of milk

2 pints of water

bread crumbs

Put the milk and water into a saucepan with sufficient salt to flavour it; place it on the fire, and, when it boils quickly, drop in the macaroni. Keep the water boiling until it is quite tender; drain the macaroni, and put it into a deep dish. Have ready the grated cheese, either Parmesan or Cheshire; sprinkle it amongst the macaroni and some of the butter cut into small pieces, reserving some of the cheese for the top layer. Season with a little pepper, and cover the top layer of cheese with some very fine bread crumbs. Warm, without oiling, the remainder of the butter, and pour it gently over the bread crumbs. Place the dish before a bright fire to brown the crumbs; turn it once or twice, that it may be equally coloured, and serve very hot. The top of the macaroni may be browned with a salamander, which is even better than placing it before the fire, as the process is more expeditious; but it should never be browned in the oven, as the butter would oil, and so impart a very disagreeable flavour to the dish. In boiling the macaroni, let it be perfectly tender but firm, no part beginning to melt, and the form entirely preserved. It may be boiled in plain water, with a little salt instead of using milk, but should then have a small piece of butter mixed with it.

Time: 1 1/2 to 1 3/4 hour to boil the macaroni, 5 minutes to brown it before the fire.

Sufficient for 6 or 7 persons.

Seasonable at any time.

Note: Riband macaroni may be dressed in the same manner, but does not require boiling so long a time.

# FRENCH FRIES

LET THE SKY RAIN POTATOES.

—William Shakespeare, *The Merry Wives of Windsor*

**IT'S A FACT**: Americans love the spud. According to the United States Department of Agriculture (USDA), Americans consume almost 130 pounds of potato a year—over 50 percent of which is consumed as french fries, chips, and other potato products. While the stats are impressive, it's not the consumption rate but the unlikely rise from detested edible to beloved icon that makes this a truly American snack.

The potato is a native of the Andes mountains and has been cultivated by humans for over seven thousand years. Spanish conquistadores first brought the nutrient-packed tuber (any fleshy root capable of reproducing without pollination) back to Europe in the mid-16th century, where it enjoyed a less-than-glorious welcome.

Peasants and the general masses or Europe were initially distrustful of the dirt-covered (and non-too-attractive) vegetable. After all, how could you trust a food that was never mentioned in the Bible? The aristocracy, however, was less concerned about the religious validity of their palates. As a result, the spud began appearing as a superficial addition to royal gardens across Europe. Royals and other government officials recognized the potential in cultivating the nutritious staple (potato spuds require a minimal amount of land to yield a full crop). Yet it wasn't until the wars and famines of the 17th and 18th centuries that farmers across Europe began to rely heavily on the potato as a staple crop.

The French royal family was one of the first in Europe to take an active role in promoting potato planting. (Marie Antoinette even wore the purple potato flower as a decoration in her hair on more than one occasion.) In 1802, Thomas Jefferson served a dinner with "potatoes served in the French manner," though it is highly unlikely that this refers specifically to what we now call french fries. Various recipes for cooking, carving, cutting, and crafting potatoes spread across Europe and America in the 19th century. Though no one is exactly sure, most historians agree that it is in this murky period of potato acceptance that the "french fry" was first invented . . . in Belgium.

According to popular legend, the french fry became popular in the United States after American soldiers returned home from fighting in WWI. The servicemen first encountered the tasty treat while liberating small towns in Northern Europe from German occupation. The citizens were speaking French, the crispy spuds were delicious— and the fact that the Americans were actually in Belgium didn't seem to bother anyone. (Belgian journalist

**THE DEVIL'S IN THE DETAILS**

Ketchup is the ubiquitous topping to french fries—so much so that sales of restaurant fries actually boosts sales of ketchup. But there are many ways to enjoy your *pomme frites*, including with mayonnaise, mustard or malt vinegar (very European), melted cheese with or without chili (oh so American) or brown gravy and cheese curds (Canadians call it poutine). You can dip them in blue cheese or Thousand Island dressing, guacamole, or carne asada.

Jo Gérard claims that his countrymen were frying potato strips as early as 1680 while Spain was in control of the area.) This linguistic fumble accounts for the fact that Americans are the only ones who refer to strips of deep-fried potato as "french." In England, fries are called "chips" (chips are "crisps" in case you were wondering); in France they are called *frites* or *pomme frites*.

In 1923, fourteen-year-old John Richard Simplot left school and began working on a farm just outside of Delco, Idaho. Shortly thereafter, Simplot became a potato man. Simplot began processing and selling his spuds across the United States. By World War II he had become the biggest shipper of fresh potatoes and was selling millions of pounds of product to the military. Spurred by wartime shortages and the need for storage, Simplot's company scientists began perfecting dehydration techniques while trying to find a way to freeze potatoes effectively. In 1953, Simplot patented the first frozen french fry and began marketing in the United States. By the late 1960s, Simplot had perfected his frozen fries and he approached McDonald's with an idea. Up to that point, all McDonald chains had been cutting and frying fresh potatoes, which led to quality control issues during the summer months. The McDonald's company struck a deal in which Simplot would supply all frozen fries to the fast-food chain franchises. And the rest, as they say, is history. Delicious, golden history.

## { FRIED POTATOES }

from *Mrs. Lincoln's Boston Cook book* (1884)

| Bacon fat or salt pork | Potatoes |
| --- | --- |

Cut cold boiled potatoes into slices about a quarter of an inch thick. Have a frying-pan hot and well greased with bacon fat or salt pork. Cook the potatoes in the fat until brown, then turn, and brown the other side.

# CAESAR SALAD

**WHAT GARLIC IS TO SALAD, INSANITY IS TO ART.**

—Augustus Saint-Gaudens

**IT CAME, THEY** saw it, and, man oh man, the Caesar salad conquered. There are two major conflicting stories that describe the origin of the Caesar salad. The most widely accepted tale begins in the 1920s in Tijuana, Mexico, with an empty kitchen, a few fireworks, and a man doing his best to fight the temperance movement.

According to legend, Italian immigrant and restaurateur Caesar Cardini first moved to Mexico to avoid Prohibition enforcement in the United States. While there he opened a successful restaurant with his brother Alessandro (Alex), and they began catering to the wealthy, young Hollywood crowd.

The restaurant was particularly busy on the Fourth of July in 1924. After an unexpected lunch rush and influx of hungry patrons, it became obvious that the kitchen was running out of traditional salad ingredients. However, rather than disappoint his discerning customers, Cardini took the opportunity to provide a little dramatic flair for his restaurant. He gathered together a few unique ingredients, rolled out a cart, and tossed the first "Caesar salad" at the table to keep the customer's entertained. Patrons loved the table-side entertainment, and Cardini himself reportedly tossed the greens whenever he could find the time.

In the twenties, Tijuana was a playground for the rich and famous of the West Coast (the newly emerging Hollywood crowd was particularly influential in trendsetting). With starlets and celebrities embracing this new salad craze, demand for Caesar's unique taste soon spread across the United States and the globe.

According to legend, Wallis Simpson first brought Caesar salad to Europe. After tasting the dish while on vacation in Tijuana, Simpson demanded that her chefs learn to make the distinctive dressing—often criticizing those who failed to capture the unique taste.

## THE DEVIL'S IN THE DETAILS

Julia Child went to Cardini's restaurant as a child and recalls, "Caesar himself rolled the big cart up to the table, tossed the romaine in a great wooden bowl, and I wish I could say I remembered his every move, but I don't. The only thing I see again clearly is the eggs. I can see him break two eggs over that romaine and roll them in, the greens going all creamy as the eggs flowed over them. Two eggs in a salad? Two one-minute-coddled eggs?"

By 1938, Cardini moved to Los Angeles and began marketing his unique dressing as a grocery product available in stores around the country. The same Cardini Original Caesar Dressing that was trademarked in 1948 can still be purchased today in specialty stores and through the Internet.

With a name like "Caesar," it's not surprising this salad is at the center of a controversy. Most food historians accept Cardini as the father of the salad. However, according to George Herter, the Caesar salad was first created in 1903 in Illinois. In his book *Bull Cook*, Herter claims that Italian immigrant Giacomo Junia tossed the first Caesar salad while working in the New York Café in Chicago. According to Herter, this salad was named after Julius Caesar—"the greatest Italian hero of all time."

## CAESAR SALAD

1 head romaine lettuce
2 eggs
3 cloves garlic, peeled
8 anchovy fillets
1 teaspoon Worcestershire sauce
1 teaspoon dry mustard

juice of 1 lemon
salt and black pepper
2 whole eggs
½ cup olive oil
½ cup grated Parmesan cheese
Croutons

1. Set a pot of water, large enough to hold the two eggs, to boil.
2. Meanwhile, wash and drain the lettuce, and cut the leaves into 1 1/2 inch pieces.
3. Mash the cloves against the sides of a large wooden salad bowl with the back of a wooden spoon until they begin to disintegrate. Scrape out most of the garlic, leaving behind the oil to flavor the salad.
4. Repeat the process with the anchovy, but leave the pieces in the bowl.
5. Add the dry mustard, Worcestershire sauce, lemon juice, salt, and pepper, and blend well.
6. Once the water is boiling, gently slide the two eggs into it. Turn off heat and cover pot. Leave for one minute, then remove eggs and cool in bowl of cold water.
7. Meanwhile, drizzle olive oil into dressing, whisking until dressing is emulsified and creamy.
8. To the bowl, add the lettuce, croutons, and Parmesan cheese and toss.
9. Carefully break open the eggs and release them onto the salad. Toss them together with the lettuce and dressing until everything is blended.
10. Serve immediately.

# COBB SALAD

I THINK I AM JUST GOING TO GET A COBB SALAD. I'D LIKE TO
MAKE A FEW SUBSTITUTIONS, IF THAT'S OKAY. I'LL GET . . .
NO BACON. NO EGGS. BLUE CHEESE ON THE SIDE.

—Larry David on *Curb Your Enthusiasm*

IF YOU'RE RUMMAGING through your refrigerator, you might pull together a salad just as Robert H. Cobb of the Brown Derby restaurant did on that fateful night of 1937, when his namesake salad was born. According to the restaurant, he was looking for a midnight snack and "pulled out this and that: a head of lettuce, an avocado, some romaine, watercress, tomatoes, some cold breast of chicken, a hard-boiled egg, chives, cheese and some old-fashioned French dressing. He started chopping. Added some crisp bacon—swiped from a busy chef."

The flavors worked beautifully, the mild chicken and creamy avocado offering a welcome counterpoint to the sharp cheese—blue or Roquefort—and the salty bacon.

The celery and greens add crunch and balance the richness of the other ingredients. Each piece of the salad adds its own texture and flavor to the mix; because they are chopped into small cubes, they mingle on the tongue.

One story goes that Cobb made the dish for Sid Grauman, who ran Grauman's Chinese Theatre. The next day Grauman asked for it again, dubbing it "Cobb's Salad." Another version credits Douglas Fairbanks Jr. as the muse who inspired Cobb. In either case, it became very popular in the restaurant, eventually finding a steady spot on the menu.

**THE DEVIL'S IN THE DETAILS**

More than four million Cobb salads have reportedly been served at Brown Derby restaurants. You'll know it's the real thing if it includes watercress.

The Brown Derby drew a Hollywood crowd, including Jack Warner, who allegedly sent his driver to pick up cartons of the salad. Clark Gable and Humphrey Bogart supposedly enjoyed it. It was even featured in an episode of *I Love Lucy*, ordered by actor William Holden.

The salad is not commonly tossed before it is served. The chopped ingredients are laid side by side or placed in quadrants by color. Or try stacking the ingredients in individual cylinders, as pictured here.

## COBB SALAD

1 head romaine lettuce
½ head iceberg lettuce
1 bunch watercress
2 tomatoes

2 boneless, skinless chicken breasts, poached and cooled
2 hard-boiled eggs
1 avocado
8 strips bacon, cooked until crisp

½ cup Roquefort or blue cheese, crumbled
2 tablespoons chives, chopped
Cobb salad dressing recipe follows

1. Chill large plates or one large shallow bowl.

2. Rinse the romaine, iceberg, and watercress in cold water. Pat dry. Chop into small even pieces and place on chilled serving plates. Spread out the greens so there is a thin layer. You'll place the other ingredients carefully onto this bed.

3. Cut the tomatoes in half and remove the seeds. Dice the flesh. Lay out on the greens in one strip, or in a quadrant if you prefer.

4. Follow in this same manner with the chicken, the eggs, the avocado, and the bacon, cutting each ingredient into small pieces and arranging them side by side, either in strips or in quadrants, on the greens. Make sure to leave room for the cheese, which should also have its own space.

5. Sprinkle the chives over the salad.

6. Serve the salads as is, with the dressing on the side. Toss the salad just before eating.

~~

## Cobb Salad Dressing
~~

| | | |
|---|---|---|
| 1 tablespoon mayonnaise | 1 teaspoon Worcestershire sauce | ½ cup olive oil |
| 1 teaspoon Dijon mustard | ¼ cup red wine vinegar, mixed with 2 tablespoons water | ½ cup vegetable oil |
| 1 glove garlic, minced | | salt |
| | | black pepper |

Whisk together mayonnaise, mustard, garlic, and Worcestershire sauce until smooth. Continue to whisk as you slowly add the vinegar mixture, then the two oils. Add salt and freshly ground black pepper to taste.

# DEVILED EGGS

•

**IT IS THE GREAT FAULT OF ALL DEVILRY THAT IT KNOWS NO
BOUNDS. A MODERATE DEVIL IS ALMOST A CONTRADICTION
IN TERMS; AND YET IT IS QUITE CERTAIN THAT IF A DEVIL IS
NOT MODERATE HE DESTROYS THE PALATE . . .**

—*Kettner's Book of the Table* (1877)

**SPICY STUFFED EGGS** existed in 13th-century Andalusia. But you can bet
they weren't toted around in the special plastic molds that are strictly a 21st-
century revelation. Then again, no one had ever heard the term "deviled"
at that point either. Whatever you want to call it, though, the deviled egg
has been around in different iterations for about eight hundred years. That's
pretty impressive.

One of the first recipes for stuffed, hard-boiled eggs was from a 15th-
century Italian cookbook, Platina's *De honesta voluptate et valetudine.* Here,
the yolks were mashed with raisins and cheese as well as minced herbs. Then
the egg halves were placed back together, and the entire thing fried in oil.

Cookbooks from the 16th century suggest that it was becoming
common to boil eggs, remove the yolks, mix them with spices and other
foodstuffs, and then put that egg yolk mixture back into the shells. By

the 17th century, it was the way to serve eggs, seasoned with pepper, mustard, and so forth. As the spices heated up—as in hell, as in associated with the devil—the name "deviled" started to apply.

The term "deviled," in reference to food, appeared in print in 1791, in James Boswell's famous biography of Samuel Johnson. Apparently, our man Boswell liked a repast of "devilled bones"

**THE DEVIL'S IN THE DETAILS**

These are a very popular item for church picnics. But watch out for the name—many congregations prefer to call them "stuffed eggs" or "salad eggs" or "dressed eggs."

for supper. (One can only assume they were spicy.) Any variety of dishes prepared with hot seasonings, such as cayenne or mustard, can be referred to as such. In 1820, Washington Irving used the word in his *Sketch Book* to describe a heavily seasoned, currylike meal.

In 1882, a recipe for "Devilled Eggs" appears in *Common Sense in the Household: A Manual of Practical Housewifery*. Many follow, and as time goes by, the devilish favorites take on a variety of spices, including paprika, parsley, chives, olives, anchovies, capers, and even caviar.

## ⌐ EGGS, DEVILLED ⌐

from *Cassell's Dictionary of Cookery* (1870)

Cut four hard-boiled eggs into halves. Remove the yolks without breaking the whites. Mix the yolks with a teaspoonful of anchovy sauce, a little cayenne pepper, and salt and fill the white cups with it; set them to stand, by cutting off the pointed tip, on a dish, surround them with small cress and finely cut lettuce. Time: fifteen minutes to boil eggs.

# CHOCOLATE CHIP COOKIES

SOMETIMES ME THINK, "WHAT IS FRIEND?" AND THEN ME
THINK, "FRIEND IS WHAT LAST CHOCOLATE
CHIP COOKIE IS FOR."

—Cookie Monster

**FIRST CAME THE** drink, then came the chip. All things chocolate (and therefore, arguably, all things wonderful) come from a small evergreen tree known as *Theobroma cacao*. Seeds from the cocoa tree have been cultivated and harvested by humans for over thirty-five hundred years. By the time the Spanish reached the capital city of Tenochtitlan in 1519, the Aztecs had perfected a foamy drink made of ground cocao seeds and water.

Depending on the season or festival, the Aztecs would add different spices and flavors to this culturally important beverage. Spanish conquistadores brought a hankering for this tasty treat back to Europe, and the international chocolate trade was born.

As Reay Tannahill notes in *Food in History*, "For almost 300 years after its introduction into Europe, chocolate was thought of as a drink.

Only in the 19th century was it to be mass-produced in block form for eating."

Baking chocolate was a product of the Industrial Revolution. With new machinery available, chemists and scientists were able to find a way to separate cocoa oil from cocoa solids during the grinding process. By the mid-19th century, chocolate bars were being munched on and baked with across Europe and America.

It was one of these edible candy bars that would revolutionize the culinary cookie world almost eighty years later in a little house just outside of Wakefield, Massachusetts.

## THE DEVIL'S IN THE DETAILS

Recently, it's come to light that allowing chocolate chip cookie dough to rest for twenty-four to seventy-two hours makes for better cookies as it allows the dough to dry out a bit as the flour soaks up the liquid of the eggs. The firmer dough is a better consistency for baking—chewy interior with a bit crispness to the exterior. Funny enough, a little research reveals that in her *Toll House Cook Book* (1953), Ruth Wakefield also recommends resting the dough in the refrigerator overnight.

In 1930, Ruth Graves Wakefield and her husband purchased an 18th-century house and decided to open an inn. The house had once served as a coaching stop for weary travelers looking to change horses and eat a warm meal. In honor of the house's past, Wakefield decided to name her new home the Toll House Inn.

A former dietitian and graduate of the Framingham State Normal School Department of Household Arts, Wakefield knew her way around a kitchen. She was known for her home-cooked meals and desserts created especially for her guests. According to culinary-lore, the chocolate chip cookie was born one day when Wakefield ran out of baker's chocolate meant to flavor her "butter drop" cookies. Instead, she grabbed a chocolate bar that was lying about her kitchen, cut it into chunks, and plopped them in her dough. The surprise came when the cookies were finished baking—the chocolate had not melted the way normal baker's bars would. Instead, the chunks had merely softened while the cookie baked around them.

The unexpected treat was a huge hit. Demands for Wakefield's dessert spread throughout New England, and soon the Toll House chocolate chip cookie was born. In 1939, Nestlé introduced its "semi-sweet chocolate morsels" as a way to make cookie baking easier on the thousands of Americans who craved chocolate chip cookies.

# ICE CREAM SUNDAE

MY ADVICE TO YOU IS NOT TO INQUIRE WHY OR WHITHER,
BUT JUST ENJOY YOUR ICE CREAM WHILE
IT'S ON YOUR PLATE.

—Thornton Wilder

**OH, THE GLORY** of the ice cream sundae. Scoops of frozen creamy custard topped with hot fudge, caramel, strawberry toppings are then adorned with a swirl of whipped cream, nuts, and the ubiquitous "cherry on top." The various components work together beautifully. You've got the icy cream melting under the warm sauce, the airy poof of sweet whipped cream, the crunch of roasted nuts, and the contrasting sharp bite of the maraschino cherry.

It's probably not a surprise that more than one person vies for credit with creating such a treat. The one thing everyone does seem to agree on is that these ice cream confections were in fact served on Sunday. Apparently the name originally was "ice cream Sunday" but that was changed to be less blasphemous.

Ice cream sodas—ice cream with soda water and a drizzle of chocolate syrup—already existed on the fateful day in 1899 when the sundae may have first been tasted. Because it was illegal to serve soda water on Sundays, the man behind the counter, Edward C. Berners of Berners' Soda Fountain in Two Rivers, Wisconsin, skipped the soda and gave his customer a bowl of ice cream with syrup. The *Chicago Tribune* credits Berners with inventing the sundae, but another town makes a compelling argument that in fact Chester C. Platt was the inventor.

Ithaca, New York, has written evidence that a "Cherry Sunday" was created and being sold by 1892—An advertisement in the town paper for such. For sure, Chester C. Platt, co-owner of Platt & Colt Pharmacy, topped vanilla ice cream with cherry syrup and cherries. "Strawberry Sundays" and "Chocolate Sundays" were soon to follow.

# HOT FUDGE SAUCE

1 cup butter
1/2 cup unsweetened cocoa powder
2 cups brown sugar

1 (12 fluid ounce) can evaporated milk
1 teaspoon vanilla extract

1.  Warm butter, cocoa powder, sugar, and evaporated milk in a saucepan over low heat until you can whisk the mixture together. Let it come to a boil and boil for 7 minutes. Remove from heat.

2.  Carefully blend hot mixture with an immersion blender or whisk by hand for 2 to 4 minutes. Add vanilla as mixture begins to cool.

3.  Serve immediately. Store in refrigerator.

# CUPCAKE

**WHEN YOU LOOK AT A CUPCAKE, YOU'VE GOT TO SMILE.**
—Anne Byrn

**WOULD A CUPCAKE** by any other name still taste as sweet? It would if it was called a fairy cake. Known in England as fairy cakes for being the perfect size for a troop of fairies, this mini cake has delighted children and adults alike for decades with its sweet proportions. After all, you can have your cake and eat it—the entire thing—too.

It's thought these diminutive cakes were inspired from the British Queen cake. This early cake was similar to the pound cake and was served individually. It is believed the spongy treats hopped across the pond and entered the American kitchen as early as 1796. The mention of the first cupcake, according to *The Oxford Companion to American Food and Drink*, can be traced back to Amelia Simmons's cookbook *American Cookery*, in her recipe notation of "a cake to be baked in small cups."

The cupcake charmed bakers with its quick baking time and simple ingredients. The origin of the cupcake's name is debated, but there are two favorite theories. One refers to "old tyme" cakes that were literally baked in teacups before anyone had muffin tins. These miniature cakes were perfect for baking in kiln ovens, as larger cakes took much longer and burned more easily.

The second theory refers to measurements of the ingredients used. The cakes, sometimes referred to as number cakes, had a very memorable list of ingredients—without any weighing necessary: one cup of butter, two cups of sugar, three cups of flour, four eggs, one cup of milk, and one spoonful of baking soda.

**THE DEVIL'S IN THE DETAILS**

Cupcakes seem to be both guilt- and recession-proof. They're rich enough to satisfy a sweet tooth and inexpensive enough to be an affordable treat.

The cupcake is embracing its fifteen minutes of fame, and loving it. Popping up everywhere are bakeries entirely devoted to specialty cupcakes—feeling like a breakfast inspired cupcake complete with maple syrup frosting and crumbled bacon on top? You got it! From television shows about cupcake competitions to books on how to decorate couture cupcakes, these munchkins have dominated the dessert world in a big way.

## { EASY CUPCAKES }

| | |
|---|---|
| 1 cup butter, softened | 4 eggs |
| 2 cups sugar | 1 cup milk |
| 3 cups flour | 1 teaspoon baking soda |

1. Preheat oven to 350°F.

2. Grease and flour muffin pan (or use paper liners).

3. Place all ingredients into a bowl and beat vigorously until incorporated.

4. Evenly fill the muffin tins.

5. Bake for 15–20 minutes or until a pale golden color.

6. Cool cupcakes in tin for 10 minutes and then remove to a wire rack.

~~

### Frosting

~~

| | |
|---|---|
| 1 cup butter, softened | 2 teaspoons vanilla |
| 8 cups confectioners' sugar, sifted | 2–4 tablespoons milk |

1. In a large bowl, beat the butter until light and fluffy.

2. Add the sugar to the bowl and carefully begin to beat it into the butter. Add the flavoring and 1 tablespoon of milk to help incorporate the sugar and butter.

3. Continue to beat the mixture, adding milk as needed until the frosting reaches the right consistency.

4. Make sure cupcakes are room temperature before you frost them.

# HAMBURGER

SCARED COWS MAKE THE BEST HAMBURGER.

—Mark Twain

**RARE, WELL DONE,** covered in cheese, or slathered with ketchup—everyone has his or her own favorite way to eat a hamburger. And who do we have to thank for this delicious addition to the American diet? Kublai Khan of course!

No one knows who exactly first created ground beef, but one popular theory traces the origins back to the days when Mongol horsemen were busy invading pretty much everywhere. These horse-bound warriors would supposedly ride with raw meat beneath their saddles. After constant movement had tenderized the meat, the horsemen would eat the raw protein without having to dismount. This precursor to steak tartar eventually made its way into Russian culinary cuisine and from there on to German plates. This myth may be a bit of a stretch as the practice of mincing meat into small pieces was a well-established culinary tradition in almost every European culture. But then again, who really wants to argue with Kublai Khan?

Popular history suggests the hamburger patty made its way to the United States along with waves of German immigrants back in the mid-19th century. However, in his book *The Hamburger: A History*, Josh Ozersky points out that precursors to the modern American hamburger were popping up in English-language cookbooks as early as 1763. And the Earl of Sandwich supposedly revolutionized lunch when he paired meat with thin slices of bread back in the 18th century. However, when they got across the Atlantic, hamburgers were here to stay by the late 19th century.

Buns and burgers came together like . . . well, ketchup and fries in 1891. According to family legend and state lore, on a warm June day in Oklahoma, Oscar Weber Bilby built himself a grill, popped on some ground beef patties, and then plopped the whole delicious mess in the middle of one of his wife's famous homemade yeast buns. The creation was so popular Bilby began to share it with his neighbors every year around the Fourth of July.

The hamburger didn't acquire the American icon mantle until fast food came to roost in the early 1920s. One Walter Anderson quit his job as a fry cook in Wichita, Kansas, and founded the hamburger chain White Castle. For the most part, ground beef was still considered a necessary but unappealing evil in early 20th century. Local butchers had been known to grind up expired meat as a way to sell it past

**THE DEVIL'S IN THE DETAILS**

Even with the rise of vegetarianism, veganism, and raw food–ism, burgers beckon to all Americans. Sure, you can have some ground-up soy or bean-studded patty, but nothing hits the spot like a big, greasy burger. Have grass-fed beef if you're feeling guilty. This fact might make you limit yourself to a burger a month, though. It's estimated that we eat around fourteen billion burgers each year in the United States.

its expiration. Books like Upton Sinclair's *The Jungle* left many Americans scared and unlikely to trust mass-produced meat. Anderson took it upon himself to revise the image of the hamburger. He set up a clean shop with public demonstrations and large discounts. Within ten years, White Castle had revived the image of the hamburger and pioneered the fast-food restaurant franchise. From there the hamburger took off.

In the 1950s, chain franchises like McDonald's took the hamburger across the United States and into foreign markets as a culinary ambassador for Uncle Sam.

# PERFECT BURGERS (CHARCOAL GRILL)

2 pounds organic, grass-fed ground beef
salt and pepper

6 hamburger buns
condiments such as ketchup and mustard

1. Start the fire in the grill.

2. Meanwhile, trying to handle the meat as little as possible, form it into 6 hamburger patties. These should be about 3 ½ inches in diameter. Don't pat them too much! Sprinkle each side with salt and pepper.

3. Place patties on the grill and cook 5 minutes per side or until the middle of the patty just barely gives when you touch it.

# BAKED ALASKA

THAT IDEA WAS ALSO A POPULAR ONE IN THE 1950s. ICE CREAM PIES WERE VERY CHIC THEN, AND BAKED ALASKA ICE CREAM PIE WAS TOO SOIGNÉ FOR WORDS.

—Sylvia Lovegren, *Fashionable Food*

**THE BAKED ALASKA**, also known as the Norwegian omelet, is a confection that lives up to its name. (Pre-global warming, that is.) You take a slab of frozen ice cream, heap on a cloud of meringue, and cook it. When it's ready, the ice cream is still frozen, and the topping is touched with the golden caramel of melted sugar. Food historians believe this paradoxical treat began pleasing its adoring public sometime around the 19th century.

The baked Alaska prototype is believed to be French in origin. Food historians agree that a dish similar to the baked Alaska appeared in France around the mid-1800s. Fancy molded bombes containing frozen cream and a cake or biscuit were perfected around this time but lacked the drama of the heat.

The idea of baking ice cream in some kind of flakey crust, so as to create a hot-cold blend of texture, is believed to have first occurred to Thomas Jefferson. In 1802, Jefferson delighted his guest, Minister Manasseh Cutler,

THE DEVIL'S IN THE DETAILS

Why doesn't the ice cream melt? Believe it or not, the whipped egg whites actually insulate the frozen custard so that the heat doesn't reach it. You also have to use really, really frozen ice cream and keep the pie in the oven for a very short time.

by serving him a pudding like dish of ice cream covered in dry flakes. However, the baked Alaska that we know today may be traced back to the work of Count Rumford, or Benjamin Thompson, an American-born scientist who studied the resistance of egg whites to heat. The brown topping that resulted eventually became the baked Alaska's crowning glory.

Then again, perhaps Charles Ranhofer, head chef at New York's famed restaurant Delmonico's, played a role. It's clear he created something very similar in 1869 to commemorate the United States' purchase of Alaska. He called the dish Alaska, Florida. The name "baked Alaska" appeared in print in 1896, in The Boston Cooking-School Book, a cookbook by Fannie Merritt Farmer, which was revised and retitled *The Fannie Farmer Cookbook* in 1965.

The dish experienced a resurgence of popularity in the 1950s when ice cream pies became all the rage. Although baked Alaska is relatively easy to make, it impressed every crowd with its complex textures and sweet flavors. While this chic little dish has fallen from the spotlight today, you can often find fried ice cream in a Chinese restaurant. (Which, incidentally, seemed to be on the record books before baked Alaska and may in fact have inspired today's dessert, using a pastry shell rather than meringue.)

# $\{$ BAKED ALASKA $\}$

from *The Boston Cooking-School Cook Book* by Fannie Merritt Farmer (1896)

whites 6 eggs
6 tablespoons powdered sugar

2 quart brick of ice cream
thin sheet sponge cake

Make meringue of eggs and sugar as in Meringue I, cover a board with white paper, lay on sponge cake, turn ice cream on cake (which should extend one-half inch beyond cream), cover with meringue, and spread smoothly. Place on oven grate and brown quickly in hot oven. The board, paper, cake, and meringue are poor conductors of heat, and prevent the cream from melting. Slip from paper on ice cream platter.

# $\{$ ALASKA BAKE $\}$

from *Ice Creams, Water Ices, Frozen Puddings* by Mrs. S. T. Rorer (1913)

Make a vanilla ice cream, one or two quarts, as the occasion demands. When the ice cream is frozen, pack it in a brick mold, cover each side of the mold with letter paper and fasten the bottom and lid. Wrap the whole in wax paper and pack it in salt and ice; freeze for at least two hours before serving time. At serving time, make a meringue from the whites of six eggs beaten to a froth; add six tablespoonfuls of sifted powdered sugar and beat until fine and dry. Turn the ice cream from the mold, place it on a serving platter, and stand the platter on a steak board or an ordinary thick plank. Cover the mold with the meringue pressed through a star tube in a pastry bag, or spread it all over the ice cream as you would ice a cake. Decorate the top quickly, and dust it thickly with powdered sugar; stand it under the gas burners in a gas broiler or on the grate in a hot coal or wood oven until it is lightly browned, and send it quickly to the table. There is no danger of the ice cream melting if you will protect the under side of the plate. The meringue acts as a nonconductor for the upper part.

A two quart mold with meringue will serve ten persons.

# LOBSTER ROLL

A WOMAN SHOULD NEVER BE SEEN EATING OR DRINKING,
UNLESS IT BE LOBSTER SALAD AND CHAMPANGE. . .

—Lord Byron

**THE LOBSTER ROLL**, the pride of Maine. This classic New England dish is dependent on the fresh lobsters caught just off the coast, a reason as to why this dish is not often seen in the landlocked parts of the country. Food historians generally agree on two points concerning the lobster roll: There is no one true recipe for lobster rolls, and lobster rolls, as we know them today, are most likely a 20th-century invention because they are served on hot dog buns.

When the first settlers came to America, few recipes were brought with them on how to prepare lobster; in fact, most early Americans were wary of the creature's edibility entirely. With its hard shell, spiny legs, and eye stalks, the lobster didn't really go out of its way to sell itself. According to the *Encyclopedia of Food and Drink*, lobsters used to be so abundant along the New England coast that they washed up in piles two feet high. These early lobsters made for quite the banquet, growing up to forty or more pounds. Lobster was no longer a dish fit only for the tables of the wealthy; with its high number, lobster was being served even in the servant's quarters.

## THE DEVIL'S IN THE DETAILS

The easiest way to cook lobster is by simply boiling it. If you place a lobster in the refrigerator for a few hours before you cook it, the cold is supposed to make it a bit less conscious. Apparently, you can also hypnotize a lobster and ready it for the pot by rubbing the top of its head or its abdomen. In any case, you'll want to keep the water boiling away as you lower the lobsters in, claws-first. Hold the top down and wait 10–15 minutes or until they turn bright red. Or you can just buy the meat—many restaurants that specialize in lobster rolls actually do this too.

Americans quickly developed a taste for lobster and began harvesting and exporting their larger lobsters around Maine. Sometime after the invention of the hot dog bun around 1912, the ground was laid for lobster rolls. It's thought that the original idea for lobster rolls might have come from lobster salad being served with toast. The dish began as a roadside snack until it was added to the menu of Fred Terry's Lobster Roll Restaurant in 1966. The restaurant proudly served many Americans their first lobster roll on a warm bun with a chilled mixture of lobster, mayonnaise, celery, and seasonings. Today, this seaside dish can still be enjoyed at restaurants and seaside shacks anywhere along the northeastern coast.

## LOBSTER SALAD

from *The Evening Telegram Cook Book* by Emma Paddock Telford (1908)

Boil one large or two medium sized lobsters and pick to pieces when cold. To make the dressing for them, beat the yolks of two raw eggs with a teaspoonful salt, a pinch of cayenne, a half tablespoonful powdered sugar, and full teaspoonful mustard wet with vinegar. Add gradually and at first very slowly one cup olive oil. When quite thick whip in the strained juice of one lemon. Beat five minutes before adding two tablespoons vinegar. Just before serving add to the dressing one-quarter cup sweet cream whipped to a froth; stir all well together and into the lobster.

# CORN DOG

HE HAD NEVER SEEN A CORN DOG, MUCH LESS TASTED ONE.
IT TOOK HIM THREE QUARTERS TO EAT ONE,
AND THEN HE ATE THREE.

—Keith Jackson

**IT DOESN'T TAKE** a chef to know that food tastes better in America when it's on a stick. The corn dog is one of the most iconic American snacks to drain from the fryers of the 20th century.

A corn dog is a hot dog coated in cornmeal-based batter, deep fried, and served on a wooden stick. The hot dog entered the American diet in the late 19th century, but the ingenious corn dog did not gain popularity until just before World War II.

No one knows who dipped the first hot dog in batter and fried it. One popular legend attributes the first official corn dog creation to two brothers from Texas. Carl and Neil Fletcher introduced their "Corny Dogs" to the Texas state fair in 1942. The dogs were a huge hit and remain so to this day. However, some evidence exists to suggest that proto-corn dogs were being sold by individual vendors at ball games and on beaches as early as the 1920s.

### THE DEVIL'S IN THE DETAILS

Yes, Virginia, there is a National Corn Dog Day. In 1992, Brady Sahnow and Henry Otley were treated to a surprise meal of corn dogs by Stan Sahnow (Brady's father) while watching the NCAA basketball tournament. A yearly tradition was born and found a national audience.

No matter who began the dipping and frying tradition, the real age of the corn dog dawned in the 1930s when George and Versa Boyington opened a hot dog stand on the sand in Rockaway Beach, Oregon. The Boyingtons began experimenting with a pancake-based batter to dip and fry their hot dogs. Though the pancake-based batter technically removed the treat from the corn dog category, product recognition remained the same. The couple called their creation the Pronto Pup, and by 1941, it was a national hit. Pronto Pup soon became part of the post–World War II franchise craze. Corn dogs are now available in frozen food sections of grocery stores nationwide—as well as fresh at state fairs!

# CORN BREAD

from *Recipes Tried and True*, compiled by the Ladies' Aid Society (1894)

2 heaping cups corn meal

1 heaping cup flour

2 teaspoons baking powder

whites and yolks of three eggs beaten separately

2 1/2 cups sweet milk

1 tablespoon melted butter

1 tablespoon white sugar

1 teaspoon salt

1.  Preheat oven to 350 degrees F.

2.  Sift together the corn meal, flour, and baking powder in a large bowl.

3.  Whip the egg whites until peaks form in a large bowl.

4.  Meanwhile, mix together the egg yolks, the milk, the melted butter, sugar, and salt until smooth in a small bowl.

5.  Beat the egg yolk mixture into the corn meal mixture just until moistened.

6.  Using a spatula, fold the corn meal-egg yolk batter into the whites until thoroughly combined.

7.  Bake in a greased loaf pan for approximately 50-60 minutes or until a tester comes out clean.

## Corned Dogs

~~

1 recipe corn bread batter

8 hot dogs, diced

1.  Mix hot dogs in with batter and bake as described.

# CLAMS CASINO

●

SHE ATE SO MANY CLAMS THAT HER
STOMACH ROSE AND FELL WITH THE TIDE.

—Louis Kronenberger

**PIGS CAN'T SWIM**, and clams don't like mud, but when the two come together, it's a dish too delicious to be ignored. Clams casino is one of the most delicious and decadent treats to come out of the Roaring Twenties. A popular dish even today, the basic recipe for Clams casino consists of an open clam covered in butter, breadcrumbs, and topped with bacon. Most recipes call for baking the clams, but a few newer recipes use grilling and steaming to cook the seafood. Today, the meal is considered a tasty delicacy, which is particularly enjoyed by Italian Americans around the Christmas holidays.

So who pioneered this farm-and-sea-based revolution? That honor has been claimed by Julius Keller in 1917. According to Keller, he created the dish while working at the casino at Narragansett Pier in Rhode Island. In an age of privilege and a milieu of old money, the casino was ruled by the formidable Mrs. Paran Stevens, who could make or break members of the staff with merely a word. One day, Mrs. Stevens ordered a luncheon meal for several ladies, which had to include soft clams. Keller noticed that

Stevens had neglected to say how she wanted the clams cooked, and he took it upon himself to offer his unique recipe for the open shellfish with bacon. Mrs. Stevens approved, and a culinary legend was born.

As Lynne Olver points out in her article "The Truth about Clams Casino," Keller's own recounting of the birth of the dish may be somewhat inaccurate. Most likely, Keller had been inspired by earlier clam recipes such as "Scalloped Oysters in Shells," "Saratoga Clams," "Soft Clams, Ancient Style," and others. Still, Keller can definitely take credit for marketing and popularizing this utterly unique dish.

## THE DEVIL'S IN THE DETAILS

Humans from every sea base have been eating shellfish since the discovery of fire. The saltwater flats and soft sandy shores of New England made for a perfect breeding ground for clams. Early colonists were wary of shellfish and tended to harvest it only as animal feed rather than as a crop in itself. However, by the early 1700s, clam had become a staple of the American diet in New England.

## } SOFT CLAMS, ANCIENT STYLE {

Adapted from 1908 recipe

Wash as many large, soft clams as you plan on eating. Open them up and discard the top half of each shell. Place a knob of butter on each clam half, sprinkle with paprika and top with a small piece of raw bacon. Roast the clams in a 400 degree F oven or on a grill for about ten minutes or until bacon is cooked through.

# POPCORN

THE LAZIEST MAN I EVER MET PUT POPCORN IN HIS
PANCAKES SO THEY WOULD TURN OVER BY THEMSELVES.
—W. C. Fields

POPCORN IS MAGICAL. You start with hard little nuggets, add heat, and fireworks erupt. Each kernel is transformed into a sculptural snack ten times its original size. Called a flake in popcorn jargon, it seems to float on air. Why? The water that was in the kernel has vaporized, and the popped corn actually weighs less than the original. Imagine being the first person to discover this trick.

Apparently, it was an accident (like many good things, including the Post-it note and the chocolate chip cookie): Someone tossed a dried ear of corn into a fire in Mexico nearly five thousand years ago, and abracadabra—snack time! Corn kernels have hard moisture-sealed hulls and a dense starchy filling. When heated, the interior expands, and the pressure of the steam literally bursts the shell open.

Archeologists have determined that popcorn was regularly made in Mexico by throwing cobs on sizzling hot stones that were tended over a campfire. As the cobs popped, they shot off in various directions. It became a game to catch the popcorn.

When Cortez landed in the Americas, he noted that the Aztecs used popcorn as a symbol of goodwill and peace. It was the holiest of snacks and adorned their god Tialoc, the master of rain, fertility, and corn. By the time the pilgrims came into the scene, popcorn was spreading through all the tribes of North America. Quadequina, the brother of Chief Massasoit of the Wampanoag tribe, brought popcorn to the first Thanksgiving dinner.

Charles Cretors invented the very first patented steam-driven popcorn carts in 1893, presented at the Columbian Exposition in Chicago. These carts were quickly seen on every street following the hungry crowds. Joining Cretors at the exposition were brothers F. W. Rueckheim, with his invention of caramel corn, and Louis Rueckheim, who introduced the first recipe of the Cracker Jack popcorn. At-home versions of Cretors's poppers were not invented until 1925 and were quickly snatched up by the wealthy.

Popcorn's popularity continued to rise during the Great Depression as an affordable treat. It took center stage once movies entered the scene. But like many stars, popcorn's fame couldn't last. The crunchy snack fell out of favor in the 1950s when televisions became a regular fixture in every American home.

### THE DEVIL'S IN THE DETAILS

Cretors's machine-popped corn is a mixture of one-third clarified butter and two-thirds lard and salt. He was the first to use oil. Earlier vendors held the kernels in a wire basket over an open flame.

Hope of redemption came to popcorn in the form of the microwavable popping bag. In 1973, Lawrence C. Brandberg and David W. Andreas invented a microwavable popcorn bag that could be stored in the refrigerator to keep the kernels fresh. The bag was known as ACT I. The next obstacle the scientists tackled was making the food shelf-stable, and in 1984, ACT II bags were in supermarkets across the country.

Popcorn is more popular than ever. In America, it could only get better as new flavors such as cheese, caramel, kettle corn, jalapeño, chocolate, and others became available. Below is a classic recipe for caramel corn—the perfect combination of salty and sweet that always leaves one satisfied.

## CARAMEL CORN

| 1 1/2 cups butter | 2/3 cup corn syrup | 8 cups popped popcorn |
| 3 cups brown sugar | 2 teaspoons vanilla | |

1. Preheat the oven to 300°F.
2. Put the popcorn in a 9 x 13 nonstick baking dish and set aside.
3. Combine butter, sugar, corn syrup, and vanilla in a heavy saucepan. Slowly bring to a boil over medium heat, being careful not to let the mixture bubble over.
4. Boil the sugar mixture for 4 to 5 minutes, stirring occasionally, until the sugar has melted completely. Turn down the heat if it seems about to boil over.
5. Remove the pan from the heat and let it rest for a minute, until it stops bubbling
6. Pour mixture over popcorn and stir with a wooden spoon until the popcorn is well coated. Be careful not to touch the syrup as it will still be very hot.
7. Place the baking dish in the oven and cook for 10 minutes. Remove from the oven, stir, and place back in the oven for another 10 minutes.
8. Take the baking dish from the oven and carefully pour the candied popcorn onto a large nonstick surface or on a large piece of parchment paper.
9. Cool the popcorn without touching for at least 20 minutes or until no longer warm to the touch.
10. Break apart to serve. Store in an airtight container or plastic bag.

# BLUEBERRY MUFFIN

HE KEPT RETURNING TO THE PATHOS OF THE FACT THAT
THERE SHOULD BE A REGION OF THE EARTH WHERE
BLUEBERRY CAKE WAS UNKNOWN.

—William Dean Howells, on his first visit to New England

**THE WILD BLUEBERRY** is the official fruit of Maine, nearly a third of all cultivated berries eaten in the United States are produced in Michigan, and yet the blueberry muffin is the state muffin of Minnesota. The sad truth is that it's fairly rare to get a genuine blueberry muffin with freshly-off-the-bush berries unless it's homemade in New England. Then again, the taste of those fresh berries bursting against the buttery crumb of a sweet muffin is heightened by its scarcity.

The word "muffin" came from the old French word *moufflet* that applied to small, soft breadlike products. Yeast was used to leaven these early muffins—think English muffins—and they were more like flat rolls than what we call muffins. Later, baking powder was used to create a light and airy cake, closer to a cupcake in texture.

American muffin recipes first began appearing in cookbooks during the mid-18th century. Their quick preparation and baking time allowed

## THE DEVIL'S IN THE DETAILS

Blueberries are filled with vitamin C and antioxidants. The only rub: You have to eat quite a few muffins to get the full benefit.

them to gain popularity. By the 19th century, muffin men walked through the streets of England selling muffins around teatime. These muffins were eventually given the name "teacakes" to separate them from their breadlike forefathers.

When European immigrants came to North America and could no longer find their usual baking buddy, the bilberry, blueberries became the obvious alternative. Baking blueberry muffins became instant in the

1920s, when New Jersey local Mr. McCollum created the first muffin mix. Blueberry muffins now practically make themselves.

Though there are many mixes available, try whipping up a batch from scratch at home with the recipe that follows. If you can't get fresh wild berries, you can get good frozen wild berries that come close to approximating that delicious freshly picked burst of fruit. Make sure you don't thaw them first, though, or you'll have blueberry mush muffins!

# BLUEBERRY MUFFINS

1/4 cup sugar

2 cups flour

2 teaspoons baking powder

1/2 teaspoon salt

1/4 cup butter, melted

2 eggs

1 teaspoon vanilla

1/2 cup whole milk

2 cups fresh or
 frozen blueberries

1. Preheat oven to 350°F.

2. Grease and flour muffin pan (or use paper liners).

3. Mix sugar, flour, baking powder, and salt together in a large bowl. Set aside.

4. In a medium bowl, whisk together butter, eggs, vanilla, and milk.

5. Add the wet ingredients to the dry and incorporate together by hand, mixing as little as necessary.

6. Fold in the berries with a spatula, mixing as little as possible. If using frozen berries, add straight from the freezer.

7. Evenly fill the muffin tins.

8. Bake for 20–25 minutes or until a pale golden color.

9. Cool cupcakes in tin for 10 minutes and then remove to a wire rack.

# CORN ON THE COB

IT IS AS AMERICAN AS ANDREW JACKSON, JOHNNY
APPLESEED, AND CORN ON THE COB.

—American Saying

IF YOU CAN boil water, you can make corn on the cob. It's one American dish that is truly native. Slathered with butter and lightly salted, it's the go-to vegetable for any barbecue. When Columbus first encountered the Arawak tribe in the West Indies, he learned the word *maize*, which translates to "that which sustains us." It was first domesticated by indigenous peoples in Mesoamerica in prehistoric times. Archeologists have found the remains of early maize ears in caves near Tehuacán, Puebla (in Mexico), dating to 2750 BC. Aztecs and Mayans cultivated it in Central and Southern Mexico, and between 1250 and 1700, the Americas embraced the food.

Corn was instrumental in turning nomad tribes into agrarian societies. Early Native Americans are responsible for breeding the hardy ancestor of the corn we now eat today. Corn can be grown in a variety of climates and can be used in a variety of ways. The corn cob first reached Europe when Columbus brought it back with him to Spain after his trip to the Americas. Native Americans taught settlers the basics on how to

**✦ ✦
THE DEVIL'S IN
THE DETAILS
✦ ✦**

If the butter-and-salt classic
is becoming dull, try mixing
flavorings into your butter:
grated lime zest, ground
pecans, grated cheese, chili
powder, or minced fresh herbs
will each offer a new taste.
Street vendors in Mexico roll
grilled cobs in melted butter,
spread them with mayonnaise,
and sprinkle them with Cotija
cheese. Served with a lime
wedge, it's decadent.

plant the crop and cultivate it. Early settlers in America might not have survived if it wasn't for corn. Even now, it's the most widely grown crop in America.

By the 1960s, with the popularity of backyard barbecues, corn on the cob found its place in Americans' hearts. Of course, there are just as many ways to cook it as there are to serve it.

## ⟨ CORN ON THE COB ⟩

There is more way than one to cook a cob of corn. First method: boiling, steaming, grilling. Even within boiling, there are options. You can drop the cob into boiling water, cover, and turn the water off. Leave covered for 8 to 10 minutes. You can add a few tablespoons of sugar to the water and boil away for 8 to 10 minutes. You can soak the stripped corn in a mixture of milk, water, salt, and melted butter and steam it. You can soak the husked corn in water and grill it. You can take out the silk, lacquer the corn with flavored (or non-flavored) butter, replace the husks, and grill it. Try them all. The one thing to remember: Cook your corn as soon after picking it as possible.

# MASHED POTATOES

NOTHING LIKE MASHED POTATOES
WHEN YOU'RE FEELING BLUE.

—Nora Ephron

MASHED POTATOES ARE one of the great American comfort foods. It's ironic that the history of this fluffy and buttery dish is tied to some of the more tragic events in Irish history.

Potatoes were first grown domestically in what is now Peru, seven thousand to ten thousand years ago. When the Spanish conquered the Inca Empire, they brought potatoes to Europe in the 16th century. Mashed potatoes are thought to have come onto the scene in 1771 as part of a competition. A French army pharmacist named Antoine Parmentier convinced the French government that potatoes were edible and safe for the starving poor.

While thousands of varieties of potatoes grew in the Andes, only a few different strains were brought back with various explorers. This lack of genetic diversity among the potatoes eventually led to the entire potato crop being completely defenseless against disease. The Great Famine of 1845 was caused by a plant fungus known as blight, which wiped out whole farms in western Ireland, killing a third of the Irish population. This tragedy caused a mass emigration of Irish, hoping to start a better life in America.

With them, the Irish brought many beloved potato recipes, including that of the traditional mashed potato. Eighteenth-century American cookbooks expanded to include a wealth of potato recipes.

## THE DEVIL'S IN THE DETAILS

Warm your milk and butter before mashing them into the potatoes to improve the texture of your mashed potatoes.

Usually the spuds were boiled, added to soups or stews, sometimes fried with butter, or even baked over a fire. Before mashing, sometimes the skins were removed from the potatoes, then butter, milk, salt, or sugar—and even various other ingredients like bacon or onions—were added. By the end of the 19th century, this humble spud rose to become a member of the elite world of fine dining and haute cuisine. Even the wealthy craved the comforting tuber and dined on such dishes as potato soufflé, croquettes, and au gratin.

The first recipes found in American cookbooks during the 1880s served mashed potatoes with their jackets, or skins, on. It is not known whether this was meant as decoration or consumption. However, one of the earliest recipes calls for peeled potatoes.

# MASHED POTATOES

from *The Art of Cookery Made Plain and Eas*, by Hannah Glasse (1747)

Boil your Potatoes, peel them, and put them into a Sauce-pan, mash them well: To two pounds of Potatoes put a pint of Milk, a little salt, stir them well together, take care they don't stick to the Bottom, then take a quarter of a Pound of Butter, stir in and serve it up.

# JELL-O

**GELATIN IS THE HOLY GRAIL.**

—Wylie Dufresne

**YOU CAN SHAKE** it, mold it, stuff it full of fruit, slurp it—just about the only thing you can't do with Jell-O is bake it. With such a high level of versatility (and let's be honest, entertainment value), it's no wonder humans have been cooking with gelatin for thousands of years.

Gelatin, in its most basic form, is a collection of amino acids that have been structurally broken apart and reformed through a process of rendering. To put it simply, gelatin is that gooey stuff that floats to the top of the water whenever a collagen-rich part of an animal is boiled (collagen is mostly found in connective tissues like knuckles or hooves). Though our hunter-gatherer ancestors may not have realized it at the time, when ancient humans learned to boil, they learned to make edible gelatin. It would take a bit more time, however, before Homo sapiens mastered the art of tuning gelatin into a delicious dessert that wiggles.

Molded jellies and colorful gelatin products didn't appear in written history until the 14th century in England. Highly skilled cooks in the

**THE DEVIL'S IN THE DETAILS**

Jell-O isn't just for kids. Add vodka instead of water, and you have a distinctly adult slurp. You can layer different colors, building it up layer by layer, waiting for each one to be almost completely set before pouring on the next. You can whip nearly-set Jell-O until it's thick and fluffy—it should double in volume. And finally, feel free to fruit it up with sliced bananas, strawberries—really anything but pineapple (the enzymes won't allow the gelatin to set). Simply add the fruit to the mold once the Jell-O has thickened enough to suspend the addition within its glorious jelly.

medieval period would order servants to boil, strain, and reboil animal joints for hours at a time in order to serve delicious jellied treats at royal banquet tables. Because of the time and skill required to create these confections, gelatin desserts were enjoyed almost exclusively by the aristocracy up until the end of the 19th century.

Not surprisingly, gelatin desserts set down democratic roots here. A Peter Cooper (of Cooper Union fame) won the first U.S. patent for a mass-produced gelatin food product in 1845. Unfortunately for dessert lovers, Copper's skills were more suited towards industrialization. The gel product never took off, and jiggling desserts remained out of reach of most people for another half century.

It wasn't until 1897 that the Jell-O we know and love would be invented by a carpenter in Le Roy, New York. While trying to develop a cough remedy and laxative tea, Pearle Wait stumbled upon a recipe for powered gelatin, which could easily be made into a dessert product. According to the Jell-O Gallery in Le Roy, it was Wait's wife, Mary, who coined the dessert's now-famous name.

Wait attempted to market the product himself, but by 1899, he decided to sell his recipe to another manufacturer in Upstate New York. The recipe passed through several owners until the Genesee Pure Food Company began a major Jell-O advertising campaign in 1900. By 1902, Jell-O sales were netting a quarter of a million dollars. The famous "J-E-L-L-O" jingle first hit the airwaves when Jack Benny sang for Jell-O ads in 1934.

## CHAMPAGNE JELLY

from *The Cookery Blue Book* by the Society for Christian
Work of the First Unitarian Church, San Francisco California (1891)

1 box gelatine
1 pint boiling water
½ pint cold water
½ pint shering
1 lemon

1 lime
¾ pound sugar
1 teaspoon essence cinamon
1 pint champagne

1. Soak gelatine in cold water.

2. Add hot water, sugar, wine, lime, and lemon, and boil five minutes.

3. Add champagne and strain twice.

4. Chill until firm.

# APPLE PIE

IF YOU WANT TO MAKE AN APPLE PIE FROM SCRATCH, YOU MUST FIRST INVENT THE UNIVERSE.

—Carl Sagan

**SOURCE OF SIN** or teacher's treat—apples are without a doubt one of the most versatile fruits on the planet. Though it's estimated that there are over 2,500 varieties of edible apples grown in the United States today, none are native variety. When the Pilgrims first arrived to settle Massachusetts Bay Colony, the only apples they found were small, sour crab apples. Colonists were forced to request cuttings and seeds from England. Once the cargo arrived, apple crops quickly flourished across the colonies.

Pies were present in 14th-century England, but they were far different from what we call a pie today. For one thing, the crust—called a coffin—was generally not meant to be eaten. In addition, sugar was scarce, so the pies weren't as sweet as those today. The oldest English-language recipe for apple pie is found in *The Forme of Cury: A Roll of Ancient English Cookery*. Complied around 1380, the recipe calls for apples, pears, figs, and raisins to be mixed and then cooked in the "coffin."

By the 16th century, sugar was commonly available, and the pastry was closer to what we have today. These recipes were brought to America with the pioneers. Recipes for apple pie continued to appear more and more often and have become a staple of American desserts. It's also become an American icon, with sayings such as, "American as apple pie," or "for Mom and apple pie," the stock answer for why soldiers were going to war in WWII.

### THE DEVIL'S IN THE DETAILS

Pie à la mode came about in the mid-1890s. A professor by the name of Charles Watson Townsend ordered ice cream with his pie regularly at the Cambridge Hotel in Washington County, New York. One day, a diner asked him what it was called. When he said it didn't have a name, she declared it pie à la mode. Soon thereafter he ordered "pie à la mode" at the Delmonico's restaurant in New York City. The waiter hadn't heard of it, so Townsend enlightened him. A reporter from the *New York Sun* heard the exchange and wrote about it the next day. It was put on the menu, pronto!

# { APPLE PIE }

from *American Cookery* by Amelia Simmons (1796)

Stew and strain the apples, to every three pints, grate the peel of a fresh lemon, add cinnamon, mace, rosewater and sugar to your taste—and bake in paste No. 3.

~~

## A Buttered Apple Pie

~~

Pare, quarter, and core tart apples, lay in paste No. 3. Cover with same; bake half an hour, when drawn, gently raise the top crust, add sugar, butter, cinnamon, mace, wine, or rosewater.

~~

## Paste No. 3 (pie crust)

~~

To any quantity of flour, rub in three fourths of its weight of butter, (12 eggs to a peck) rub in one-third or half and roll in the rest.

# STEAK

·····•·····

**MY FAVORITE ANIMAL IS STEAK.**

—Fran Lebowitz

**CHRISTOPHER COLUMBUS BROUGHT** steak to the New World. Really. Most die-hard steak lovers would be loath to hear it, but beef is not an American birthright. It originated in Spain, and it was brought here—by here, we mean Hispaniola—by ship on Columbus's second voyage. The cattle not only survived the 3,400-mile voyage, but they thrived on the land. In 1519, Hernando Cortez took offspring of these cattle to Mexico to set up ranches. Often the cattle roamed wild and later came to the United States by way of Texas and California.

Cattle were brought to Jamestown in 1607, but none survived. It was a disastrous time, with few supplies and much hardship, so when more appeared in 1611, Governor Thomas Dale issued a proclamation: "No man shall dare kill any bull, cow, calf . . . whether his own or appertaining to another man." It seemed to help—by 1620, there were five hundred cattle and by 1639, thirty thousand—and beef was on the table.

The late 1800s saw an America without buffalo; the Native Americans had been pushed out to reservations, farms had been established, and the railway was opening up the cattle industry. In 1871, a Detroit meat packer named G. H. Hanharmand brought refrigeration railway cars west, allowing cattlemen to bring their animals-turned-steaks from the West to the busy, beef-hungry East.

Beef grew in popularity and became a status symbol for American tables after World War II. Steak continues to be a beloved favorite of Americans everywhere. The perfect New York strip steak is defined by the

### THE DEVIL'S IN THE DETAILS

Manhattan's first cattle appeared in 1625. The Dutch settlers wanted to protect their farms and cattle from the Native Americans and wild animals, so they built a wall— and that's where the name of Wall Street originated.

contrast between the charred exterior and the warm, juicy center. This cut is a favorite of New Yorkers and America alike because of its amazing flavor and tenderness. Breaking it down, the strip is cut from the short loin, which consists of a muscle that is relatively unused. The strip is cut loose from any bones, which differentiates it from a T-bone steak.

# ⎰ TO BROIL A BEEFSTEAK ⎱

from *The Century Cookbook* by Mary Ronald (1901)

Time: one inch thick, eight minutes; one and a half inches thick, ten minutes.

Trim a steak into good shape, taking off the end-piece to be used in some other form, as it is not eatable when broiled; take off superfluous fat; make the surface smooth by striking it with the broad blade of knife; heat the broiler very hot. Take a piece of the fat, trimmed off the meat, on a fork and grease the broiler well; lay on the steak with the outside or skin edge toward the handle, so the fat may run on the meat. Place it close to the hot coals and count ten slowly; turn it and do the same; this is to sear the outside and keep the juices in; then hold it farther from the coals to cook more slowly, and turn it as often as you count ten, counting about as fast as the clock ticks. If turned in this way very little fat will run into the fire, and it also cooks slowly, giving an even color all through. The flame from fat does not injure the meat, but the smoke must be avoided. Wrap a napkin around the hand holding the broiler to protect it from the heat. A steak ought not to be less than an inch, but should be one and a half to one and three quarters inches thick. Allow eight to ten minutes for cooking according to the thickness. One two inches thick will take fourteen to eighteen minutes. A steak should be rare but not raw, should have a uniform red color, and be full of juice.

When done it will be puffed between the wires of broiler, and will offer a little resistance to the touch. If experience does not enable one to judge in this way, remove the broiler to a dish on the table, and make a small clean cut on one side. Do not at any time pierce the meat with a fork. Sprinkle it with salt and pepper, and spread with maitre d'hotel butter. If the steak has to stand a few minutes before serving, which should be avoided if possible, dredge it at once with salt and pepper, but do not spread with the maitre d'hotel butter until just before sending it to the table. The heat of the meat must melt the butter, and the parsley should look fresh and bright. Steak, as well as all broiled articles, should be garnished with slices of lemon and with water-cress.

Fried potato-balls, straws, puffed, or Saratoga potatoes may be served on the same dish.

# POTATO SALAD

FOUND A LITTLE PATCHED-UP INN IN THE VILLAGE OF
BULSON. PROPRIETOR HAD NOTHING BUT POTATOES; BUT
WHAT A FEAST HE LAID BEFORE ME. SERVED THEM IN FIVE
DIFFERENT COURSES-POTATO SOUP, POTATO FRICASSEE,
POTATOES CREAMED, POTATO SALAD AND FINISHED WITH
POTATO PIE. IT MAY BE BECAUSE I HAD NOT EATEN FOR
36 HOURS, BUT THAT MEAL SEEMS ABOUT THE BEST
I EVER HAD.

—General Douglas MacArthur

**THE FIRST WRITTEN** notation of a potato salad appeared in 1597, when a chef named John Garrard writes about dressing roasted in oil, vinegar, and salt.

Because potatoes were eaten the world over, they have been immortalized in a dozen different salad variations. German potato salad is prepared as a warm salad with a sweet-and-sour dressing made from sweetened vinegar with bits of ham and bacon. Greek potato salad also uses warm boiled potatoes but adds lemon juice and olive oil to the mixture. A cold potato salad with vinaigrette and fresh tarragon hails from France, and the British also served theirs cold.

The idea of using mayonnaise—as well as adding chopped hard-boiled eggs, sweet gherkins, onions, and whatever other embellishments the American palate craved—was something wholly unique to the American potato salad.

In 1886, Juliet Corson (social activist and founder of the New York Cooking School) published *Miss Corson's Practical American Cookery and Household Management*. The book contained two recipes for "potato salad" and was one of the first publications to identify a distinctly "American potato salad."

## THE DEVIL'S IN THE DETAILS

The best potatoes for potato salad are the waxy types such as Yukon Gold, red potatoes, and any small boiling potatoes. Many recipes recommend peeling and tossing the warm cooked potatoes with your dressing of choice. This will assure a nice layer of seasoning on each piece of potato—the dressing soaks in a bit, making a lovely salad.

## AMERICAN POTATO SALAD

from *Miss Corson's Practical American Cookery and Household Management* (1886)

Peel half a dozen cold boiled potatoes and slice them, not too thin; boil two eggs hard. Wash, and chop rather fine, one head of celery; peel one onion, and chop it fine. Break the yolks of the hard-boiled eggs, smooth with the yolk of one raw egg; stir with them a gill of oil, two tablespoonfuls of vinegar, a level teaspoonful each of salt and dry mustard, and a saltspoonful of pepper. Mix this dressing with the potato, celery, and onion, and serve the salad.

# PUMPKIN PIE

THREE CHEERS NOW, EVERYBODY! LET THE ECHOES REACH
THE SKY!

IN HONOR OF THAT UNKNOWN SOUL WHO FIRST MADE
PUMPKIN PIE!

MY EYE!

DELICIOUS PUMPKIN PIE!

OH MY!

—*Boy's Life*, November, 1917

IF IT'S TOO small to take to the ball, then it's the perfect size for a pie. Pumpkins are one of those delicious and versatile agricultural products that have come to represent America at its tastiest.

Indigenous to North America, pumpkins were first introduced to Europeans by Native Americans living in the northeast section of the continent. Gourd cooking was already established throughout Europe, and ships quickly brought back the tasty orange gourd back across the Atlantic sometime in the early 16th century.

Some historians claim cooking with the *pampion* was a technique that arrived in England via France; others claim the culinary tradition was a direct import from English colonists in the New World to countrymen back home. Either way, the first "pumpkin pies" were actually a type of poor man's stew, which involved using the orange gourds themselves as the cooking pot. A hungry cook would cut off the top of the pumpkin, scoop out the seeds, and throw in whatever tasty ingredients he or she wanted to slow-roast. Afterward, the pumpkin would be placed directly in the smoldering ashes of a cooking

**THE DEVIL'S IN THE DETAILS**

Most canned pumpkin is actually squash—a mix actually of butternut, Hubbard, and other squashes. The texture and consistency of the squash is actually better for canning purposes, and the taste is nearly identical to that of the pumpkin.

fire, where it would sit until the outer shell was completely black. A little scoop, a little time, and voilà, pie without the pan!

The earliest recipe for a pumpkin pie in England was penned by Hannah Woolley in 1675; across the pond a century later, Amelia Simmons included a recipe in her cookbook, *American Cookery*, the first known cookbook written by an American.

## POMPION PYE

from *The Gentlewoman's Companion* by Hannah Woolley (1675)

Take a pound of Pompion, and slice it; an handful of Time, a little Rosemary, sweet Marjoram stripped off the stalks, chop them small; then take Cinamon, Nutmeg, Pepper, and a few Cloves, all beaten; also ten Eggs, and beat them all together, with as much Sugar as you shall think sufficient; then fry them like a Froise; and being fried, let them stand till they are cold; Then fill your Pye after this manner: Take Apples sliced thin round-wise, and lay a layer of the Froise, and another of the Apples, with Currans betwixt the layers; be sure you put in good store of sweet Butter before you close it. When the Pye is baked, take six yolks of Eggs, some White-wine or Verjuice, and make a Caudle thereof, but not too thick; cut up the lid and put it in, and stire them well together whilst the Eggs and Pompions are not perceived, and so serve it up.

## POMPKIN PIE

from *American Cookery* by Amelia Simmons (1796)

No. 1 One quart stewed and strained, 3 pints cream, 9 beaten eggs, sugar, mace, nutmeg and ginger, laid into paste No. 7 or 3, and with dough spur, cross and chequer it, and baked in dishes three quarters of an hour.

No. 2 One quart of milk, 1 pint pumpkin, 4 eggs, molasses, allspice, and ginger in a crust; bake 1 hour.

# PEANUT BUTTER

**MAN CANNOT LIVE BY BREAD ALONE;
HE MUST HAVE PEANUT BUTTER.**

— James A. Garfield (U.S. President)

**WHETHER YOU'RE FIRMLY** in the crunchy camp or a staunch supporter of smooth, there's no arguing over the fact that peanut butter is one of the most delicious and beloved American foods. It's estimated that U.S. citizens consume around seven hundred million pounds of the pasty snack every year.

Archaeological evidence suggests that peanuts originated somewhere in South America near Peru or Brazil. The small legumes were introduced to Africa, Asia, and Europe through Spanish traders, though the exact pattern of dispersal remains murky. In the United States, peanuts remained a largely ignored food until the food shortages caused by the Civil War. Soldiers and civilians alike would scrounge for the tiny "groundnuts" to stave off hunger. After the war, peanuts returned to relative obscurity until the late 1800s when a new wave of vegetarianism became popular among health reformers.

In 1897, Dr. John H. Kellogg received the first patent for a peanut-grinding method issued in the United States. At the time, Kellogg had been working with his brother (and future founder of the Kellogg cereal company), Will Keith, to try and develop more a nutritional meal for the residents of the Battle Creek Sanitarium. Dr. Kellogg was a major advocate for vegetarianism, and he wrote extensively about the benefits of cereal grains, fruits, and nuts. He was also militantly determined that the only acceptable way to make peanut butter was to avoid roasting the nuts at all costs.

At the same time that Dr. Kellogg was saving morales and nutrition in Michigan, an unknown physician in St. Louis, Missouri, was supposedly working on a way to create a nutritious food source to help people who couldn't chew meat due to bad teeth. The details get a little murky here, but the peanut paste recipe eventually wound up in the hands of George A. Bayle Jr., who "began selling peanut butter out of barrels for about 6¢ per pound."

While medicine spurred the creation of peanut butter, it was George Washington Carver's work at the Tuskeegee Institute that truly paved the road to a peanut-butter-loving nation. Carver spent forty-seven years

THE DEVIL'S IN THE DETAILS

Dr. John H. Kellogg insisted that roasted peanut butter is not wholesome. His method was to essentially boil the nuts, as follows: "Remove the skins, as I have explained; then take the nuts, with an equal quantity of water, and put in a covered dish; set it in the oven, and let them bake for several hours. If the nuts get too dry, add a little water, and cook until the water is evaporated. Rub the cooked nuts through a colander, add a little salt if you like, and you have the most delicious nut butter you ever tasted in your life. It is perfectly digestible, too."

working to improve Southern farming techniques and to educate poor farmers. In the early 20th century, boll weevil beetles devastated the already-declining cotton industry in the Southern United States. Over the course of his career, Carver created over three hundred peanut-based products (food and household necessities). Through dissemination of free brochures and traveling with his demonstration lab (known as the Jessup wagon), Carver ushered in the age of peanut farming in the South.

As Carver experimented with peanuts in his lab, Americans were experimenting in their kitchens. Definitely a precursor to the enduringly popular PB and J.

## FRUIT SANDWICHES

from *The Boston Cooking-School Cook Book* by Fannie Merrill Farmer (1896)

Remove the stems and finely chop the figs. Add a small quantity of water, cook in a double boiler until a paste is formed, then add a few drops of lemon juice. Cool mixture and spread on thin slices of buttered bread; sprinkle with finely chopped peanuts and cover with pieces of buttered bread.

# KEY LIME PIE

•

IF I WERE ASKED TO NAME THE GREATEST OF ALL REGIONAL
AMERICAN DESSERTS, MY ANSWER MIGHT VERY WELL BE
*KEY LIME* PIE . . .
—Craig Claiborne

**IT'S SAID THAT** necessity is the mother of invention, but in the case of the Key lime pie, invention is the mother of deliciousness.

The first piece of the puzzle, which is the creamy sweet-tart custard pie, involves condensed milk. Until the completion of the Florida Overseas Railroad in 1912, the archipelago known as the Florida Keys was accessible only by ship and small boat. Household refrigerators hadn't yet been invented, so nonperishable condensed milk (a product that had just been invented by Gail Borden Jr. in 1856) was the only "milk" available in the keys.

The second piece is the small citrus fruit found only in the Florida Keys, a fruit brought to the islands by Spanish explorers sometime in the 16th century. Key limes are smaller, juicier, and have thinner skins than their more common counterparts, the Persian limes.

No one is sure exactly who came up with the idea of mixing sweetened condensed milk with citrus juice. It was apparently fairly common in the keys—after all, the limes were on the trees and the cupboards held the canned milk.

Popular legend attributes the dish to the mysterious "Aunt Sally" who lived and worked for William Curry in the late 1800s. Curry, a Bahamian immigrant and salvage magnet, was Florida's first millionaire. He hired Sally as a cook, and shortly thereafter, she perfected the citrus dessert from recipes that were already floating around the fishing communities of Key West.

## THE DEVIL'S IN THE DETAILS

The acid in the lime juice reacts with the milk to thicken the mixture. Much like the citric acid in a seafood seviche, the juice actually warms up and cooks the substance. Many early recipes didn't require any cooking of the pie. But with concerns about consuming raw eggs at a premium, most of the pies served today spend a bit of time in the oven.

In 2006, the key lime became the official pie of Florida, deftly defeating its rival, pecan pie, for the lofty position. It continues to be enjoyed nationwide, although oftentimes regular old limes have to be used. The topping is traditionally a meringue, but whipped cream can also be used. If you want to really raise the bar, try it with vanilla ice cream.

# ⟨EASY KEY LIME PIE⟩

1 (9-inch) graham cracker pie crust

1 (14-ounce) can sweetened condensed milk

4 egg yolks, beaten

½ cup Key lime juice (or regular lime juice)

Whipped or ice cream, for serving

1.  Preheat oven to 350°F.

2.  Whisk together the condensed milk and egg yolks.

3.  Slowly add the lime juice, whisking as you do. The mixture should begin to thicken.

4.  Pour into the prepared graham cracker pie crust.

5.  Bake for about 15 minutes or until filling is almost set. Do not brown the pie.

6.  Refrigerate until chilled .

7.  Serve with whipped cream or ice cream.

# SOFT PRETZELS

These pretzels are making me thirsty.

—Kramer on *Seinfeld*

**THE MOST POPULAR** rumor in the historical pretzel debate claims that the salty snacks were first created sometime around 610 CE in either Northern Italy or Southern France. A monk supposedly took bits of leftover dough from the kitchen and twisted the ropes into a set of praying arms. The baked snack served as both a way to teach prayers and to reward small children who would be fed the treat. The name "pretzel" comes from the Latin word *pracatio* which means "prayers."

The pretzel may have been made by those who pray, but its universal appeal meant that it was quickly adopted by those who fight.

One popular pretzel legend states that in 1510, Turks from the Ottoman Empire were yet again laying siege to the city of Vienna. In an attempt to break the stalemate, the Turks began digging tunnels under the city walls at night with the hope of creating a surprise attack. Vienna's bakers were early risers, and on their way to the shops, they detected the heinous plot and alerted the city's military. After saving the day, the bakers received a special coat of arms from the people of Vienna. This heraldic reward can be seen today as most bakeries in Germany and Austria have a plaque that shows two lions standing to the left and to the right of a giant soft pretzel.

A suspiciously similar rumor puts the story in the 1600s and says that the bakers of Vienna created the "croissant" as a dessert celebrating the defeat of the Turks (hence the crescent shape of the pastry). It's possible that bakers saved Vienna twice, or the two stories might have become blended in the historical ethos. Either way, munching on a pretzel seems like a pretty good way to celebrate victory.

**THE DEVIL'S IN THE DETAILS**

The distinctive shiny brown coating of an authentic German soft pretzel comes from a dip in lye, the story of which reveals yet another accidental success. Apparently, a German baker was carrying a tray of uncooked pretzels to the kitchen when he dropped them into a vat of lye solution—used to clean and disinfect baking utensils. He decided to bake them anyway. The result was a distinctive color and tang.

In Europe, soft pretzels had become mostly associated with German and Austrian cuisine. Not surprisingly, the tasty snack arrived in the United States along with waves of German immigrants sometime in the mid-19th century. The first commercial pretzel bakery in the United States was established in 1861 in Litiz, Pennsyvania, where it still operates today as the Julius Sturgis Pretzel Bakery. According to the Sturgis legend, the company recipe was a gift from a grateful traveling hobo who received a warm meal and friendly welcome from Julius Sturgis himself back in 1851.

Sturgis's snack was a huge success, and pretzel factories soon began blooming across Pennsylvania and the United States. In 1933, the Reading Pretzel Machinery Company introduced the first automatic pretzel-twisting machine, and the pretzel business was off and running.

# ⟨ SOFT PRETZELS, MADE WITHOUT LYE ⟩

1 package active dry yeast
1 c warm water (approximately 115 degrees F)
2 ½ - 3 cups bread flour

1 tablespoon vegetable oil
2 tablespoons vegetable oil
6 tablespoons baking soda
Coarse sea salt or kosher salt

1.  Dissolve yeast in water.

2.  In a large bowl, combine 1 ½ cups flour and sugar. Mix in the yeast and water, and oil, and beat for about 3 minutes or until smooth. Gradually add enough additional flour until a soft dough forms and the dough is no longer sticky.

3.  Turn dough out onto floured surface and knead until smooth, about five minutes.

4.  Put dough in large bowl greased with a small amount of vegetable oil. Turn over so top of dough is greased as well. Cover tightly with plastic wrap and let rise in a warm place until doubled, about 1 hour.

5.  Deflate dough by punching it down, turn out onto floured surface and cut into 12 pieces.

6.  Roll each piece in a ball and then a smooth rope about 18 inches long. Twist each rope into a pretzel shape and set aside.

7.  Let pretzels rise until puffy, about 25 minutes.

8.  Meanwhile, bring about 6 cups of water to boil in a 3-quart stainless steel pot. Dissolve baking soda in water and keep water at a simmer.

9.  Grease a large baking sheet and set aside. Heat oven to 425 degrees F.

10. Using a slotted spoon, float 1 pretzel at a time into the water. Let simmer for 10 seconds, then flip to the other side. Simmer another ten seconds, then remove from water and let drain on drying rack. Repeat with all pretzels.

11. Place pretzels on greased baking sheet.

12. Bake for 12-15 minutes or until golden.

# BROWNIES

THE SUPERIORITY OF CHOCOLATE, BOTH FOR HEALTH AND
NOURISHMENT, WILL SOON GIVE IT THE SAME PREFERENCE
OVER TEA AND COFFEE IN AMERICA WHICH IT HAS IN SPAIN.
—Thomas Jefferson

**INSPIRED BY CANADA** but made in America, brownies are a North American masterpiece. The first brownie recipe appeared in Fannie Farmer's *Boston Cooking-School Cook Book* in 1896. Farmer named her recipe after the popular *The Brownie* cartoons and poems created by Canadian-born writer Palmer Cox. The literary Brownies were small, mischievous, and charmingly benign fairies that were a favorite among children across the United States. Oddly enough, this very initial recipe did not contain a shred of chocolate! In 1905, however, Farmer reworked her recipe, this time adding chocolate.

Or so one legend goes . . . Another suggests that brownies were actually created in the early 1890s at the behest of Chicago socialite and philanthropist Bertha Honoré Palmer. Palmer was on the Ladies Board of Managers for the World's Colombian Exposition of 1893 held at the Palmer House Honoré. She supposedly requested a dessert for ladies that was easier to eat than a piece of pie and smaller than a of layer cake could be served in boxed lunches. The chefs returned with brownie squares. The same tale also claims that the first reference to this dessert as a browine actually occurred in a Sears Roebuck catalog from 1898.

In any case, Maria Willett Howard (a protégé of Farmer's) published a recipe for chocolate brownies in 1912. The recipe is named after the second largest city in Maine, contributing to the other popular rumor that brownies were created by a Bangor housewife rather than Farmer.

## THE DEVIL'S IN THE DETAILS

Most brownies have roughly the same ingredients: Chocolate, butter, sugar, eggs, and flour. Sometimes nuts. Yet by changing up the proportions, every baker makes the brownie her own. Sometimes a brownie contains three different kinds of chocolate, from unsweetened, to cocoa, to semi-sweet. The amount of butter and flour can vary dramatically. Chocolate frosting or ganache can gild the lily. It's interesting to note that one of the first recipes—that of the Palmer House Hotel—offers an orange gelatin-based topping. The hotel still serves the very same brownies as it did in 1893.

# BANGOR BROWNIES

Adapted from *Lowney's Cook Book* by Maria Willett Howard (1912)

¼ cup butter

1 cup brown sugar

3 squares of unsweetened chocolate

1 egg, beaten

½ cup of flour

1 cup chopped nut meats

1. Preheat the over to 350°F. Grease and flour an 8-inch square baking pan.

2. Place the butter, chocolate, and sugar in the top of a double boiler. Over simmering water, melt the butter and chocolate and stir in the sugar until incorporated. Remove from heat.

3. When the chocolate mixture is cool to the touch, whisk in the egg, until just incorporated.

4. Mix in the flour and nuts, again being careful not to overmix.

5. Bake for 20 minutes, or until just set. The middle of the brownies should still look a bit soft.

6. Cool in the pan.

# DOUGHNUTS

BETWEEN THE OPTIMIST AND THE PESSIMIST, THE
DIFFERENCE IS DROLL. THE OPTIMIST SEES THE DOUGHNUT;
THE PESSIMIST, THE HOLE.

—Oscar Wilde

**SUGAR AND FAT.** What could be more American?

Almost every culture has developed some tradition of frying dough and cooking grain in fat. Modern Americans tend to think of the word "doughnut," and a soft, crispy round confection pops to mind. The closest ancestors to these circular treats were first created in the Netherlands. According to the *Oxford Companion to Food and Drink*, *ollekoecken* were a favorite Christmas treat for the Dutch. The sticky fruit-filled dough would be plopped off a spoon into a pan of heated oil. The fried confections would take a round shape, similar to today's beignets.

Crullers share the same Dutch origins as the doughnut. The only major difference between the two was the shape the dough took on when cooking in the oil. The Dutch brought their holiday confection to the New World, where the culinary tradition quickly blended with similar recipes from other immigrant cultures. Industrialization aided the doughnut explosion. Machines for frying, poking, and cutting the confectionary treats were patented across the United States. John F. Blondel of Thomaston, Maine, invented a machine with a spring-loaded tube that would push the dough out of the cake's middle in 1872. By the late 19th century, doughnuts were firmly enmeshed in the American diet.

Estelle Woods Wilcox recorded her preferred recipe for "Crullers" and "Fried Cakes" in *Buckeye Cookery*. In the age before cholesterol scares, Wilcox edifies her readers that "clarified drippings of roast meat are more wholesome to fry them than lard." She dictates further, "Fry in an iron kettle, the common skillet being too shallow for the purpose. Do not eat doughnuts between April and November. Crullers are better the day after they are made."

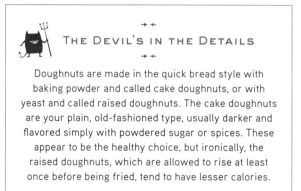

+ +
## THE DEVIL'S IN THE DETAILS
+ +

Doughnuts are made in the quick bread style with baking powder and called cake doughnuts, or with yeast and called raised doughnuts. The cake doughnuts are your plain, old-fashioned type, usually darker and flavored simply with powdered sugar or spices. These appear to be the healthy choice, but ironically, the raised doughnuts, which are allowed to rise at least once before being fried, tend to have lesser calories.

The story of the doughnut is delicious, but the myths of the hole are charming. No one really knows who first hollowed out the center of the doughnut, but it seems likely that a Captain Hanson Crockett Gregory invented them while frying up a mess of doughnuts aboard ship. In an interview he gave the *Washington Post* on March 26, 1916, he explains,

Now in them days we used to cut the doughnuts into diamond shapes, and also into long strips, bent in half, and then twisted. I don't think we called them doughnuts then—they was just "fried cakes" and "twisters."

Well, sir, they used to fry all right around the edges, but when you had the edges done the insides was all raw dough. And the twisters used to sop up all the grease just where they bent, and they were tough on the digestion.

Well, I says to myself, "Why wouldn't a space inside solve the difficulty?" I thought at first I'd take one of the strips and roll it around, then I got an inspiration, a great inspiration.

I took the cover off the ship's tin pepper box, and—I cut into the middle of that doughnut the first hole ever seen by mortal eyes!

Well, sir, them doughnuts was the finest I ever tasted. No more indigestion—no more greasy sinkers—but just well-done, fried-through doughnuts.

In 1921, a Bulgarian immigrant named Arnold Levitt invented a machine that could mass-produced doughnuts. His Donut Corporation of America, founded just after World War II, helped bring the doughnut worldwide acclaim. In 1950, the first Dunkin' Donuts opened in Quincy, Massachusetts; and by the late 1990s, Americans were eating an estimated ten billion doughnuts every year.

## CRULLERS

from *Buckeye Cookery and Practical Housekeeping:
Compiled from Original Recipes*, edited by Estelle Woods Wilcox (1877)

Six eggs, one cup-coffee sugar, six table-spoons melted butter, four of sweet milk, one tea-spoon soda in the milk, two tea-spoons cream tartar in the flour, one tea-spoon ginger, half a small nutmeg (or any other seasoning), flour to roll out; fry in hot lard. If the lard is not fresh and sweet, slice a raw potato, and fry before putting in the cakes (Miss. M. B. Fullington).

# CEREAL

LIKE RELIGION, POLITICS, AND FAMILY PLANNING,
CEREAL IS NOT A TOPIC TO BE BROUGHT UP IN PUBLIC.
IT'S TOO CONTROVERSIAL.

—Erma Bombeck

**LIKE MANY A** great American institution, breakfast cereal came into being at the lucky confluence of religion, capitalism, and the pursuit of a healthy bowel movement.

Whether you start your day with organic, all-natural, high-fiber, multigrain granola pellets or prefer super honey-chocolate-dipped high-fructose flakes, your morning ritual must give a nod to the Dansville Sanitarium in New York, the birthplace of a concoction called granula, as well as the Seventh-Day Adventist Church and its pursuit of a purer, more vegetarian religion.

In 1863, Dr. James Caleb Jackson developed the first American breakfast cereal, and he called it granula. This twice-baked concoction of bran nuggets may have been extremely healthy, but tasty it was not. Granula was so hard it had to be soaked, usually overnight, before it could be consumed. While Dr. James Caleb Jackson's granula is indisputably the first American breakfast cereal, it would be another thirty years before a more palatable option was developed.

Dr. John Harvey Kellogg (the name gives it away, doesn't it?) was also seeking to develop a healthier breakfast option for his patients at his sanitarium in Battle Creek, Michigan. Creating a high-fiber breakfast cereal was no small task—problems with the bowels were often a major reason for a retreat to a sanitarium, and the doctors had to find a solution. Following the lead of Sister Ellen G. White (a patron of Jackson's sanitarium before founding the Seventh-Day Adventist Church, of which Kellogg was a devout member), Kellogg and his brother, Will, created a variation of granula made from dried and crumbled biscuits of bran, oats, and corn or wheat meal. By all accounts, it too was not particularly tasty.

But then, in 1894, the brothers Kellogg managed to stumble upon a flaky version of their corn cereal. After accidentally leaving a sheet of wheat grain out overnight, the frugal pair decided to run the wheat through the oven (despite its staleness), to see if they could salvage any grain. What came out were small yellow flakes of corn and wheat grain. Lo and behold, Kellogg's Corn Flakes and the modern American cereal industry were born. Dr. Kellogg continued to focus on his work in the medical field, and by 1906, Will bought out his brother and became the sole proprietor of the Battle Creek Toasted Corn Flake Company.

Will Kellogg's company soon had a fierce competitor on the market—Charles William Post, enamored with the healthy cuisine

### THE DEVIL'S IN THE DETAILS

A New York City pastry chef, Christina Tosi, invented "cereal milk" to use in her much-lauded dessert menu. She toasts corn flakes, soaks them in milk before straining out the cereal and flavoring the milk with sugar and salt. It's doubtful that Dr. Kellogg would approve.

he had tried as a sanitarium patient in Battle Creek, launched Grape-Nuts and Post Toasties under his Postum brand in 1895. Post quickly mastered the art of advertising cereal. With his unique marketing campaigns, he set the groundwork for creating one of the largest cereal companies in the United States.

In a world where cereal marketing is aimed squarely at young children, featuring television characters on the outside of the boxes and highly processed nuggets of sugar on the inside, many people are turning back to a style more like granula.

## HOMEMADE GRANULA

from *Miss Corson's Practical American Cookery* (1886)

Granula, as sold at the shops, is rather expensive and can be prepared at home with but little trouble; it is excellent for gruels and porridges for invalids and children.

To prepare the granula, use stale pieces of graham or brown bread; cut the stale bread in pieces of equal thickness, put them into the oven, and bake them until they are light brown then roll them with a rolling pin until they break into small crumbs. Sift the crumbs through a coarse sieve to ensure uniformity, rolling and sifting again the crumbs too large to pass through the sieve the first time; keep the granula in airtight jars or boxes in a dry place and use it as required. It will keep as well as cracker-dust. Any of the recipes for preparing gruels and panadas will serve for the preparation of granula, or it may be used to thicken hot milk or soup for invalids or children.

# BAGEL

THE BAGEL IS A LONELY ROLL TO EAT ALL BY YOURSELF BECAUSE IN ORDER FOR THE TRUE TASTE TO COME OUT YOU NEED YOUR FAMILY.

ONE TO CUT THE BAGELS, ONE TO TOAST THEM, ONE TO PUT ON THE CREAM CHEESE AND THE LOX, ONE TO PUT THEM ON THE TABLE AND ONE TO SUPERVISE.

—Gertrude Berg

**YOU CAN SMEAR** it, smother it, cover it in butter, or just go au naturel and toast it. However you choose to dress your breakfast treat, bagels are one of the most popular breakfast foods in the American diet.

At its most basic, the bagel is a round piece of dough that has been boiled and baked to create that "soft on the inside and chewy on the outside" effect. No one quite knows the true origin of the bagel. Most cultures have been cooking with yeast-based grain products for thousands of years (archaeological evidence even suggests round roll-like bread with holes in the middle were first created in ancient Egypt). However, popular tradition suggests modern bagels can trace their origins back to Eastern Europe sometime in the 16th or 17th century.

This circular piece of perfection first made its way across the Atlantic in the 19th century when Jewish immigrants began pouring into the eastern seaboard of the United States en masse. The round treats were so popular that in early 20th century, Bagel Bakers Local 338 formed in New York City. Meetings were initially held in Yiddish, and all bagels were hand-rolled and cooked.

In the post–World War II era, bagels began to spread across

**THE DEVIL'S IN THE DETAILS**

In 2004, Bruegger's Enterprises set the world record for biggest bagel ever baked. The 868-pound bagel measured six feet across and was unveiled at the New York State Fair.

the United States—frozen bagels were introduced to grocery stores in the 1950s. Bagel-making machines began to pop up across the United States in the 1960s, largely driving out the handmade traditions that had previously dominated the bagel market. One patent from 1966 read, "It is an object of this invention to provide a machine wherein bagels are cooked automatically and without human supervision." By 1970, Bagel Bakers Local 338 had been driven out of existence.

Mass-produced though it may be, the bagel is here to stay. By 1995, Americans were spending more than $1.5 billion a year on bagels.

# ⌐BAGELS AND LOX⌐

Fresh bagels
Lox (cold-smoked salmon)
Cream cheese (plain or with chives)
Capers, drained

Tomatoes, sliced thin (optional)
Cucumbers, sliced thin (optional)
Red onions, diced

1. Slice bagels and toast right before serving.

2. Spread about 1 tablespoon cream cheese on each bagel half.

3. Sprinkle capers over cream cheese. Press lightly to secure.

4. Top with 1 slice of tomato, if using.

5. Top with cucumbers to cover, if using. (One layer).

6. Top with 1-2 slices lox, draped in half to cover bagel.

7. Sprinkle with red onions.

8. Serve immediately.

# ICED TEA

———●———

**ICED TEA IS TOO PURE AND NATURAL A CREATION NOT TO HAVE BEEN INVENTED AS SOON AS TEA, ICE, AND HOT WEATHER CROSSED PATHS.**

—John Egerton

**IS IT** "ice tea" or "iced tea?" That depends on where you live. In the South, the chilled beverage is called ice tea. Everywhere else, it's "iced."

Iced tea did not take its current form until the popularity of black tea took off, thanks to the work of the Indian Tea Commission at the St. Louis World's Fair in 1904. As the legend goes, Richard Blechynden, the head of the commission, watched the fairgoers pass by his elaborate teahouse as the sweltering temperatures made hot beverages unpalatable. Driven to increase the market for Indian black tea in the States, he hit upon the idea of not only serving it iced but also perhaps more importantly, giving it away for free. His booth was soon the most popular at the fair as the patrons found his golden beverage to be the perfect refreshment.

Spurred on by his success in St. Louis, Blechynden toured the country, giving away more and more iced tea, quickly spreading its popularity nationwide. Brewing the perfect iced tea at home, complete with sweet and often fruity syrups, soon became the hallmark of a great hostess. Iced tea was mixed with all sorts of flavors in delicious punches: lemon, mint, strawberries, cherries, and oranges, whether fresh, preserved, or in syrup form or, for the more mature palette, brandy and bourbon to give it a little extra kick. And though few still have time for such an elaborate

## THE DEVIL'S IN THE DETAILS

Use double the amount of tea or teabags that you would use for hot tea when you're planning to chill the drink. And allow the tea to come to room temperature before you put it into the refrigerator. Fill an ice cube tray with tepid tea and freeze for ice that won't dilute your drink. You could also float some minced mint or fruit in the cubes for a special treat.

and time-consuming production (early recipes recommend beginning to brew tea at breakfast for service at dinner), iced tea remains an American favorite, available in bottles, cans, and even from a soda fountain.

#  RUSSIAN ICED TEA

from *The International Jewish Cook Book* by Florence Kreisler Greenbaum (1919)

Make tea for as many cups as desired; strain and cool. Place in icebox; chill thoroughly and serve in tall glass with ice and flavor with loaf sugar and one teaspoon preserved strawberries, raspberries, cherries, or pineapple—or loaf sugar may be flavored with lemon or orange and packed and stored in jars to be used later to flavor and sweeten the tea. Wash the rind of lemon or orange and wipe dry, and then rub over all sides of the sugar.

#  ICE TEA WITH GINGER ALE

from *For Luncheon and Supper Guests* by Mrs. Alice Bradley (1923)

1 quart fresh cold water

4 individual tea bags or 4 heaping Orange Pekoe tea

large piece of ice

1 quart ginger ale

Sugared lemon slices

Bring water to boiling point. Add tea bags. Cover and let stand 2 minutes. Strain over a large piece of ice. Just before serving add ginger ale. Serve with sugared lemon slices.

~~

## Sugared Lemon Slices

2 large lemons

6 tablespoons sugar

Cut lemons in slices and lay on a plate. Sprinkle with 4 tablespoons sugar. Turn over and sprinkle with 2 tablespoons sugar. Just before serving arrange lemon on lemon plate with lemon fork. Put any extra syrup into the tea. Use one or more slices lemon in each glass of tea.

# PANCAKES

OF A CERTAIN KNIGHT, THAT SWORE BY HIS HONOR
THEY WERE GOOD PANCAKES, AND WORE BY HIS HONOR
THE MUSTARD WAS NAUGHT. NOW I'LL STAND TO IT, THE
PANCAKES WERE NAUGHT, AND THE MUSTARD WAS GOOD,
AND YET WAS NOT THE KNIGHT FORSWORN.

—William Shakespeare, *As You Like It*

**THE OLDEST WRITTEN** record of a these tasty treats comes from a fragment of Greek comedic writing from about 500 BC. "And a pancake hot and shedding morning dew" was salvaged from the comedic writings of an Athenian citizen named Cratinus. No one knows the exact context in which the sentence was placed, but Cratinus was most likely referring to *tiganites*, or "Greek pancakes." *Tiganites* are generally more fried than grilled, but the thin batter and cooking directions are almost identical to other pancake recipes from around the world.

As the Greeks munched on *tiganites*, the French created *crêpes*, the Russians devoured *blinis*, and in India, *puda* was snacked on by all. In Scotland, pancakes were generally left to rise higher than in the rest of Europe. Sweet butter or honey was usually placed on top of the cooked snack rather than mixed into the uncooked batter or used as filling later.

Yet there be any question of the authenticity of American pancakes, it is certain that Native Americans cooked coarse cornmeal cakes on skillets. These led to flapjacks, which were popular in colonial America.

There are almost as many kinds of pancakes as people. For the most part, differences in thickness and rising agents are the result of geographic availability. Culturally, the major differences between pancakes around the world are the toppings. Not surprisingly, the American toppings tended to be sweet—most notably, maple syrup, a quintessentially American topping. Regions that favored thinner cakes tend to use the cooked dish as a wrapping for other ingredients.

### THE DEVIL'S IN THE DETAILS

Pancakes are best piping hot, just off the griddle. With that in mind, it's always best to make them fresh, and there are many mixes on the market if you don't have time to make yours from scratch. You can get your standard mix, to which you'll add egg, water, or milk and oil. You can get a complete mix, to which you need only add water. Either way, let your batter sit for at least fifteen minutes if you can wait. The result will be better, lighter pancakes.

## FINE PAN-CAKES FRYED WITHOUT BUTTER OR LARD

from *The Compleat Cook* by Nathaniel Brook (1658)

Take a pint of Cream, and six new laid Egs, beat them very well together, put in a quarter of a pound of Sugar, and one Nutmeg or a little beaten Mace (which you please) and so much flower as will thicken almost as much as ordinarily Pan-cake batter; your Pan must be heated reasonably hot & wiped with a clean Cloth, this done put in your Batter as thick or thin as you please.

## PAN CAKES

from *The Frugal Housewife* by Susannah Carter (1803)

Take a pint of thick cream, six spoonfuls of sack, and half a pint of fine flour, six eggs, but only three whites, one grated nutmeg, a quarter of a pound of melted butter, a very little salt, and some sugar; fry these thin in a dry pan.

# CHICKEN-FRIED STEAK

"THIS IS SO GOOD, IT JUST SCREAMS AMERICA."

Paula Deen, tasting her Chicken Fried Steak.

**SOME CALL IT** country, some call it chicken, but either way, there's no denying this fried steak is delicious! CFS is a regional dish that has been popular in the Southern and Western United States since the mid-19th century. The basic meal consists of a tenderized piece of steak battered and fried in oil. Most recipes don't consider the meal complete unless the steak is then smothered in gravy and potatoes.

Like so many other foods in the American lexicon, CFS is a product of European influences meeting local resources. Some culinary experts claim CFS can be traced back to German and Austrian immigrants who arrived during the first half of the 19th century with recipes for "wiener schnitzel." This tasty dish is created when a thin piece of meat (usually veal) is dipped in egg, coated in bread crumbs, and fried.

Beef was far more available and popular than veal in America, especially in the wilds of Texas where cattle was the linchpin of most homesteads. Homemade recipes for fried steak began popping up in communities across the United States.

Joe Yonan in the *Washington Post* (June 25, 2008) offered a number of theories as to where chicken friend steak originated, including one of the charming accidental variety.

> The story tells of Jimmy Don Perkins, a short-order cook at a cafe in Lamesa (even farther west than San Angelo), who on one fateful day in 1911 wrongly assumed that a waitress's ticket for two orders ("chicken, fried steak") was for only one. He had never heard of it, but figured the only way to make it was to cook the steak like fried chicken. So that's what he did.

He goes on to quote "the venerable Texas food authority Robb Walsh," who offers the origins of three separate types of CFS: From Southern fried chicken came the East Texas CFS, dipped in egg and then flour; the weiner schnitzel connection led to the Central Texas version, which uses bread crumbs in the flour mixture; and the common cowboy favorite, pan-fried steak, is most similar to the eggless West Texas CFS.

## THE DEVIL'S IN THE DETAILS

Chicken-fried steak is beef steak fried up like fried chicken. So is country-fried steak. Except when it's chicken. Then it's chicken-fried chicken. Steak-fried chicken can be breaded and fried boneless pork chops. Or chicken breast or steak. One thing's for sure: It will be served with gravy. Either milk or brown.

# GUMBO

**TASTE AND RIVALRY!** Few dishes can claim to inspire as much passion as the epic soup-stew hybrid gumbo. Chicken versus seafood! Hot versus mild! There are literally thousands of ways to cook and enjoy this traditional Southern treat. In 2010, Tabasco even sponsored the 21st Annual World Championship Gumbo Cookoff. The event lasted three days and had over five different winning categories.

For all the versatility of gumbo, one factor remains constant: okra. A tropical plant native to the Congolese region of Africa, okra arrived in the Americas as a result of the massive slave trade taking place during the 16th and 17th centuries. In Africa, okra was often used as a thickening agent in soups and stews. Some food connoisseurs claim that the tradition of incorporating okra in soup sprouted upward, as slaves in the Louisiana region taught Creoles and plantation owners to add the plant to their culinary repertoire. Others claim that okra had been a part of French cooking long before slaves commandeered that plant.

On the website What's Cooking America, Mark W. Huntsman provides a detailed look at Louisiana gumbo:

> Because gumbo has been a staple in Louisiana kitchens long before written records of the dish existed, there are many myths surrounding its origins. No one is even certain whether the dish is Cajun or Creole in origin—the oldest mention to date is when French explorer C.C. Robin ate it at a soiree on the Acadian coast in 1803. Yet there are records of New Orleans creoles enjoying it during roughly the same time period.
>
> The oldest records I have found that describe the contents of gumbo are from *Pavie in the Borderlands: The Journey of Theodore Pavie to Louisiana and Texas, 1829-1830, Including Portions of His* Souvenirs atlantiques by Betje Black Klier, where he mentions consuming "lots of squirrel gumbo, a delicious stew made with rice and Chateaubriand's sassafras."

As early as 1885 there were writers who recognized gumbo as the culinary legacy of the African American community. Although the French contributed the concept of the roux and the Choctaw invented filé powder, the modern soup is overwhelmingly West African in character. Not only does it resemble many of the okra-based soups found in contemporary Senegal, the name of the soup itself is derived from the Bantu words for the okra contained within—*guingombo tchingombo or kingombo*. A legacy of the colonial era, the modern French word for okra is quite simply *gombo*).

Additionally, Jessica B. Harris has found Afro-Caribbean soups with similar compositions and names to their Louisiana counterpart. The recipe she gives in *Iron Pots & Wooden Spoons: Africa's Gifts to New*

*World Cooking* reads like a modern Louisiana gumbo: onion, celery, a ham hock, a bay leaf, etc.

Most likely, gumbo is the result of combined influences and regional availability. Gumbo was the perfect basic stew, which could be spiced up with leftover ingredients and seasonal proteins. Each chef could truly make it his or her own.

## THE DEVIL'S IN THE DETAILS

Okra is a distinctive-looking vegetable with an equally distinctive texture. It produces a sticky juice that thickens stews and gumbos naturally, which is why you can't have gumbo without okra. It looks like a long fuzzy pod and can grow up to seven inches long. Originally grown in Northwest Africa, it traveled to Brazil in the 1600s and to North America with the slave trade.

## GUMBO

from *Directions for Cookery in its Various Branches* by Eliza Leslie (1840)

Take an equal quantity of young tender ochras, and of ripe tomatas, (for instance, a quarter of a peck of each.) Chop the ochras fine, and scald and peel the tomatas. Put them into a stew-pan without any water. Add a lump of butter, and a very little salt and pepper; and, if you choose, an onion minced fine. Let it stew steadily for an hour. Then strain it, and send it to table as soup in a tureen. It should be like a jelly, and is a favourite New Orleans dish. Eat dry toast with it.

# MEAT LOAF

•

HOT, MEATY, ECONOMICAL, IRREVOCABLY ASSOCIATED WITH
FAMILY LIFE AND WOMEN'S HOME COOKING, MEATLOAF—THE
HUMBLE GI OF THE MEAT WORLD—KEPT THE FLAG FLYING ON
THE KITCHEN FRONT AND KEPT THE FAMILY SUPPLIED WITH
COMFORT FOOD.

—Sherrie A. Inness, *Cooking Lessons*

**FOR SOME, IT** is a comfort, a reminder of the easy days of childhood and the
delicious reliability of Mother's home cooking. For others it is a dreadfully
heavy culinary heap, the dried-out husks of yesterday's dinner, and a sign that
all of the good, fresh food is gone. But love it or hate it, meat loaf is a dish
ingrained within the consciousness of American cuisine, a reminder of its
efficiency, resilience, and almost endless adaptability. Ground meat mixed
with various grains or vegetables, a variety of spices, and perhaps an egg or
wine to bind it together, and then shaped like bread and baked, topped with
sauce or gravy, or maybe bacon and mashed potatoes—meat loaf is a heavy
dish, a filling dish, one that has taken leftovers and cast-off ingredients and
made them seem plentiful to generations of American eaters.

Minced meat dishes in various forms, from meatballs to meat pies to
dishes resembling meat loaf, have been around as long as recipes have been

recorded. The Roman cookbook *Apicius De Re Coquinaria*, which dates from AD 4th or 5th century, includes an entire chapter devoted to minces, with a recipe for Aliter Isicia Omentata, or "Another Kind of Kromeskis," which closely resembles meat loaf.

Their European ancestors have continued the legacy: The Danes serve *forloren* topped with bacon strips, boiled potatoes, brown sauce, and red currant jelly; eat German *Hackbraten*, Hungarian *Stefània szelet*, Italian *polpettone*, Jewish *Klops*, Romanian *drob*, or Bulgarian Rulo Stefani; and you may find boiled eggs inside your loaf. The Arabian world serves the heavily spiced *kofta*, and in the Philippines, you can order *embotido* filled with carrots and eggs, steamed in banana leaves, then fried for breakfast.

The American version of meat loaf did not appear until the technological advances of the Industrial Revolution made ground meat readily available in the market. The earliest recipes for meat loaf appear in the 1880s. These recipes from the turn of the century were frequently developed in test kitchens at industrial giants, who were eager to sell their ground meat products to a wary public. One of the more popular recipes at the time called for the use of oatmeal, specifically manufactured by Quaker Oats.

It took the lean years of the Great Depression to make meat loaf a staple of the American diet. Subsisting on less meant stretching food, especially more expensive meat products. Thus, dishes that

## THE DEVIL'S IN THE DETAILS

Meat loaf has always been an extremely flexible dish—for some of us, it is a comfort food covered with bacon or potatoes and slathered with gravy, tomato sauce, or even ketchup; for others, it represents a way to make red meat more lean and nutritious by adding shredded vegetables to the mixture. It appears on trendy fine-dining menus as well as those at roadside diners.

called for cutting meat with cheap grains became an economic necessity. Meatloaf not only allows for stretching meat but can also accommodate leftovers and scraps of just about anything, reducing waste and budget strain. The dish remained popular during the prosperous 1950s, as housewives appreciated not only its efficiency but also its ease—meat loaf takes little time to prepare and even less attention as it cooks.

## VEAL LOAF

from *Mrs. Lincoln's Boston Cook Book* (1884)

Parboil two pounds of lean veal. Chop fine with one fourth of a pound of salt pork or bacon; add four butter crackers, pounded, two eggs, well beaten, two teaspoonfuls of salt, one saltspoonful of pepper, and half a saltspoonful of nutmeg or mace. Moisten with the meat liquor, mould into an oval loaf, and put into a shallow tin pan. Add a little of the water in which the meat was boiled. Bake till quite brown, basting often. Serve hot or cold, cut in slices. Raw veal may be used in the same way, baking it two hours or more.

# REUBEN SANDWICH

THE HELL I WILL. I'LL CALL IT A REUBEN'S SPECIAL!

—Arnold Reuben (*allegedly*)

**THE MYTH, THE LEGEND**, the Reuben! In its most basic form, the Rueben sandwich layers corned beef with swiss cheese, sauerkraut, and dressing on toasted rye. Regional variations between Thousand Island dressing and Russian dressing exist, and of course, the great "to mustard or not to mustard" debate rages across Formica tables to this day.

Who was the genius behind such a unique mix of ingredients? It's almost as if someone carrying a hot dog with ketchup and sauerkraut ran into someone with a pastrami on rye, hold (or not) the mustard. History has yet to pick a clear winner.

According to some sources, the Rueben sandwich was first created in Omaha, Nebraska, by a grocery storeowner named Reuben Kulakofsky. Kulakofsky apparently created the dish as part of his contribution to a weekly poker tournament held in the mid-1920s. One of the players happened to be Charles Schimmel, owner of the Blackstone Hotel. Schimmel supposedly placed the sandwich on the hotel's lunch menu, and voilà—instant success.

Other culinary sources scoff at Nebraskan pride and instead claim that the Rueben sandwich is a native New York invention. The earliest New York claim dates back to just before World War I. Patricia Taylor, daughter of the famous New York restaurateur Arnold Reuben, stated that her father created the sandwich late one night when a hungry actress wandered into his deli and asked for a unique creation of leftovers. Annette Seelos supposedly took one bite and begged to have the late-night snack named in her honor. Maybe she didn't tip well, or maybe Arnold just wasn't a fan of her work; but either way, it's been known as the Rueben ever since.

To this day, New Yorkers and Nebraskans continue to vie for the honor of calling the Rueben sandwich their own. Culinary historians on both sides of the debate have called for evidence using everything from oral histories to old menus. One fact that has remained undisputed is that by the mid-1950s, the Reuben sandwich had come to reign supreme on the American lunch palate. In 1956, Fern Snider took first place at the Wheat Flour Institute's inaugural National Sandwich Idea Contest in Omaha, Nebraska. Her entry? The Reuben sandwich. Her prize? A trip to New York City.

## { REUBENS FOR TWO }

4 pieces rye bread
Russian or Thousand Island dressing
8 pieces corned beef

4 pieces swiss cheese
½ cup sauerkraut,
  drained well

1. Lightly toast the rye bread.

2. Spread a thin layer of dressing on each slice, then place them side by side, dressing side up.

3. Divide the meat and cheese up and layer on the bread to make two sandwiches. Make sure the top layer is the meat.

4. Put about half of the sauerkraut on each sandwich. Top with the bread, dressing side down.

~~

### Russian Dressing

~~

Mix equal amounts ketchup and mayonnaise. To make this into Thousand Island, add a spoonful of pickle relish.

# TUNA FISH SALAD

IS THIS CHICKEN, WHAT I HAVE, OR IS THIS FISH? I KNOW
IT'S TUNA, BUT IT SAYS "CHICKEN OF THE SEA."

—Jessica Simpson

**HUMANS HAVE BEEN** eating tuna since at least the 5th century BC when fishermen across the Adriatic and the Mediterranean would hunt the elusive, majestic fish. Tuna remained largely a delicacy until the advent of canning in the mid-19th century. Cans of tuna were first imported to the United States from Italy and France, but the price of fishing and shipping the underwater snack food prohibited consumption for the average American. More importantly, in the late 19th century, sardines were the favored choice for canned fish in the United States.

In 1903, a canner named Albert P. Halfhill noticed that the stock of sardines off the coast of San Pedro Bay in California was rapidly dwindling. In an effort to stay afloat, Halfhill turned his attention to the albacore tuna, which could be caught in large quantities off the waters of Southern California. Other canners began to mimic Halfhill's strategy and began shifting away from the sardine market. Recipes for tuna sandwiches began appearing in cookbooks as early as 1914. The biggest impetus for change came with World War I, when American soldiers abroad needed large quantities of easily transportable protein—a can of tuna would fit that bill nicely.

By the early 1920s, canned tuna fish was widely popular across the

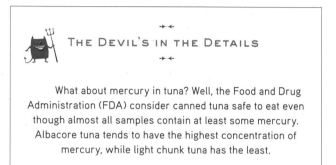

## THE DEVIL'S IN THE DETAILS

What about mercury in tuna? Well, the Food and Drug Administration (FDA) consider canned tuna safe to eat even though almost all samples contain at least some mercury. Albacore tuna tends to have the highest concentration of mercury, while light chunk tuna has the least.

United States. The healthy and comparatively cheap food was in even more demand during the Great Depression, when the price of meat was far above what most Americans could afford. As a result, tuna fish sandwiches graced the lunches of many a baby boomer throughout their formative years.

Made with mayonnaise and occasionally brightened with chopped celery, pickles, or dried mustard and lemon juice, tuna salad was commonly served between slices of white bread or on lettuce leaves. For a special treat, the sandwich was toasted with cheese.

The tuna melt remains one of the most popular dishes on diner menus to this day.

## TUNA SANDWICH

from *The Neighborhood Cook Book* (1914)

Shred the contents of one can of Pierce's brand of Tuna fish, add finely chopped celery, green pepper, olives and nuts; mix with mayonnaise, placing crisp lettuce leaves between thin slices of bread and spreading the mixture upon them.

## TUNA SALAD

| | |
|---|---|
| 1 can oil packed tuna fish | lettuce |
| 1 can water-packed tuna fish | salt and pepper |
| ¼–½ cup mayonnaise | |

1. Open both cans of tuna fish. Drain oil and water. Squeeze excess water out of water-packed tuna fish. Put in medium-sized bowl.

2. Mix fish with mayonnaise. Adjust to taste.

3. Add salt and pepper.

4. Serve on lettuce leaves.

# MAYONNAISE

································●································

MAYONNAISE: ONE OF THE SAUCES WHICH SERVE THE
FRENCH IN PLACE OF STATE RELIGION.

—Ambrose Bierce

**LOVE TO HATE** it, or hate to love it—mayonnaise is one of those fundamental sauces that has helped to define American cooking in the 20th century. This delicious—and occasionally fluffy—condiment can trace its origins back to 18th-century France.

According to culinary legend, mayonnaise was first created as a celebratory dish following the conquest of the tiny island of Minorca, which exists a few miles off the coast of Sicily. Back in 1756, France and Great Britain were yet again engaged in one of their ever-so-frequent wars for continental power. The Seven Years' War had just kicked off, and Spain thought this would be a great time to try to get the tiny island they had lost to Great Britain almost fifty years earlier. French and Spanish forces had overrun the entire island except for the tiny holdout town of Port Mahon. The Duke of Richelieu arrived on Minorca in the spring and immediately tried to take down the small British fort. Richelieu's siege lasted for almost two months before the fort finally surrendered.

### THE DEVIL'S IN THE DETAILS

As with most historic recipes, it's almost impossible to know the real story. However mayonnaise was first created, it quickly became a staple of high cuisine in France. Mayo's arrival in the United States is even less certain; however, by the late 19th century, cookbooks across the United States had recipes for mayonnaise sauce.

To celebrate the end of the siege, Richelieu issued orders for a banquet. His personal chef planned to include a sauce of cream and eggs as one of the many dishes to be served. However, after realizing supplies of cream were running low, Richelieu's chef substituted olive oil for cream and came up with mayonnaise!

For the most part, mayonnaise was considered a delicacy in 19th-century America and, in particular, as a great addition to salads. The price of imported olive oil made mayonnaise expensive for most home cooks. As cross-Atlantic shipping grew cheaper, and farmers in Florida and California began to produce domestic olive products, mayonnaise sauce grew in popularity among U.S. citizens of every economic background.

In 1903, Richard Hellmann arrived in the United States from Germany, and within two short years, he and his wife would revolutionize the world of mayonnaise. Hellmann's wife supposedly created a mayo sauce that was a prize feature at Hellmann's deli in New York City. By 1912, Hellmann was selling the "blue ribbon" jar by the crateload. On the other side of the country, Best Foods Inc. was creating a popular mayonnaise following in California. In 1932, the two companies merged, and an enduring and delicious mayonnaise empire was born.

## THE DEVIL'S IN THE DETAILS

How do a raw egg yolk, lemon juice, and a few tablespoons of olive oil combine to make a gorgeous creamy emulsion? The key is in adding the oil to the yolk a drop at a time, keeping the yolk moving by whisking or using a food processor. This allows the two liquids to blend together— literally dispersing and suspending tiny droplets of the oil throughout the yolk. Once you have an emulsion going, you can add the oil quicker. Then, whisk in the lemon juice or vinegar. If the mixture "breaks" back down into separate elements, you can try to fix it. Whisk a new egg yolk in a different bowl and add the "broken" emulsion drop by drop into the new yolk. It should come together again.

# MAYONNAISE SALAD DRESSING

Adapted from *Presbyterian Cook Book* of Dayton, Ohio, by Mrs. E. B. Stoddard (1873)

Into the yoke of one raw egg, stir a few tablespoons of olive oil dropped in very slowly. Continue to add olive oil a drop at a time, as much as the yolk can hold; half a pint of oil can be used. Season with lemon juice, cayenne pepper, salt, and mustard.

# FRIED CHICKEN

THE FOOD IN EUROPE IS PRETTY DISAPPOINTING. I LIKE
FRIED CHICKEN. BUT OTHER THAN THAT EUROPE IS GREAT.

—Donnie Wahlberg

**IT'S HARD TO** resist fried chicken's perfectly seasoned, crispy skin and moist interior. The dish is loved by novice cooks and professional chefs alike all over the globe. Nearly every cuisine in the world has its own recipe for fried chicken, but no area is quite as passionate about this dish as the Southern United States.

In the case of this dish, the art of frying came long before fried chicken. People have been frying all sorts of food forever in an attempt to make their meat, bread, or cheese more palatable. This was especially the case for meat; by dredging it in flour and spices before cooking, the morsel became tender, and the flavor was enhanced. Frying became a popular cooking method among ancient peoples because it was fuel-efficient and portable. Records of the frying fad go back as far as Roman times; cooking texts from this era describe recipes for both sweet and savory fritters.

When Scottish immigrants settled in the American South, they brought their own style of fried chicken—deep-frying them in fat. The first confirmed fried chicken feast was recorded in 1709 at the plantation of Govenor William Bryd II in Virginia. As Africans were brought to work on Southern plantations, they continued to perfect the dish by adding spices the Scottish recipes lacked. Fried chicken was well adapted for plantation life because it stood up well to heat and had an efficient, simple cooking process. The dish survived the end of slavery and fell into common use as a Southern staple.

The idea of frying with lard made sense in the 18th and 19th centuries, because hogs were becoming more available and bigger (bigger pigs equals more lard). Fried foods, particularly chicken, were inexpensive and substantial, a great combination for the time.

Southern fried chicken did not gain widespread popularity in America until sometime during the 19th century when chicken production became industrialized and was widely available year-round. The term "Southern fried chicken" finally appeared in print in 1925, as the dish became a Sunday-dinner regular across the country.

Health concerns have prompted more home cooks to prepare an oven-baked version of the dish. Naturally, there is a product on the market to make this even easier: Shake 'n Bake are pouches of seasoned bread crumbs and other ingredients. You simply drop the chicken pieces into the pouch, shake it up, then back the chicken on a cookie sheet. If that is too labor-intensive, there's always Kentucky Fried Chicken and Popeye's.

# FRIED CHICKEN

from *What Mrs. Fisher Knows about Old Southern Cooking* by Abby Fisher (1881)

Cut the chicken up, separating every joint, and wash clean. Salt and pepper it, and roll into flour well. Have your fat very hot, and drop the pieces into it, and let them cook brown. The chicken is done when the fork passes easily into it. After the chicken is all cooked, leave a little of the hot fat in the skillet; then take a tablespoonful of dry flour and brown it in the fat, stirring it around, then pour water in and stir till the gravy is as thin as soup.

# BISCUITS

POWDER MILK BISCUITS: HEAVENS, THEY'RE TASTY AND
EXPEDITIOUS! THEY'RE MADE FROM WHOLE WHEAT, TO GIVE
SHY PERSONS THE STRENGTH TO GET UP AND DO WHAT
NEEDS TO BE DONE.

—Garrison Keillor

**BISCUITS HAVE BEEN** a vital part of American cookery since its very beginning. A basic combination of flour, rising agent, and liquid the biscuit could be whipped up and baked off quickly and easily. Early biscuits, were usually baked twice so they would keep longer. They were flat and hard objects that did the job of filling the stomach but little else.

In the 14th century, the twice-baked biscuit was called a biscuite, derived from the Latin *bis* (twice) and *coquere* (to cook).

These biscuits could be taken to sea for long periods as they would not rot. They were cheap to make and very easy—often, they would be baked off in a cooling oven after loaves of bread were done cooking.

The definition of the biscuit varies. A biscuit in England is, and was, a cookie. Early 19th-century cooks in the northeastern United States made something similar. On the other hand, cooks in the South made fluffy, light biscuits, sometimes beating the batter for half an hour before letting the dough rest, in order to create a softer, more absorbent culinary treat.

## → ← THE DEVIL'S IN THE DETAILS → ←

When you make your biscuit with cream or butter, sugar, and even possibly eggs, you get a cakier, sweeter concoction known as shortcake. The crumbly texture of both biscuits and shortcake comes from the fact that the gluten is not allowed to develop. Baking soda, rather than yeast, is the leavening agent used to get the dough to rise.

Shortcakes or biscuits can make spectacular bases for sweetened strawberries, which became quite a hit in the second half of the 19th century, when the transcontinental railroads could transport strawberries from coast to coast on ice. Oh la la!

## AUNT FANNIE'S BUTTERMILK BISCUIT

from *America Cookery Book* by Jane Croly (1872)

Into one quart of thick buttermilk, stir enough flour to make a thick batter, add a little salt, a tea-spoonful of carbonate of soda, and a tea-spoonful of melted butter. Beat to the consistency of drop-cake, and drop a table-spoonful for each biscuit on a buttered pan. Bake twenty minutes.

## STRAWBERRY SHORTCAKE

from *The Century Cookbook* by Mary Ronald (1901)

4 cupfuls of sifted flour

3 heaping teaspoonfuls of baking-powder

1 teaspoonful of salt

1 teaspoonful of butter

1 teaspoonful of lard

milk

2 quarts of strawberries

Sift the baking-powder and salt with the flour, rub in the shortening; then with a fork stir in lightly and quickly sufficient milk to make a soft dough, too soft to roll. Turn it into a greased tin, and bake in a hot oven for thirty minutes. Watch to see that it rises evenly. Unmold, and leaving it inverted, cut a circle around the top, within one inch of the edge; lift off the circle of crust, and with a fork pick out the crumb from the center, leaving about three quarters of an inch of biscuit around the sides. Spread the inside of the cake with butter, and then fill it with crushed strawberries, which have been standing half an hour or more mixed with sugar enough to sweeten them. Turn off the juice from the berries before filling the cake. Replace the circle of crust, and cover the whole cake, top and sides, with meringue, heaping it irregularly on the top. Use a pastry-bag if convenient to give the meringue ornamental form. Place it in the oven a moment to slightly color the meringue. Arrange a few handsome berries on the top. Serve the strawberry-juice as a sauce. Whipped cream may be used instead of meringue, if convenient. Shortcake, to be good, should be freshly made, and served as soon as put together.

# CHEESECAKE

I'M QUITE PARTIAL TO MINDY'S CHEESECAKE.

—Sky in *Guys and Dolls*

ARCHAEOLOGISTS BELIEVE AN early cheese pastry was created in ancient Greece sometime before the first Olympic Games, about 750 BC. It was made from cheese pounded until smooth, with honey and wheat flour. It was fed to the athletes for strength.

One early written mention of cheesecake is found in one of Greek scholar Callimachus's many works, written around 250 BC. He suggests that a Greek physician Aegimius wrote a book about cheesecake. (Who knew?) In 160 BC, Roman politician Marcus Porcius Cato's book *De Agri Cultura* includes not one but two cheesecakes: *placenta*, which has a crust, and *libum*, which is more of a loaf. In addition to being devoured by mortals, these were used as offerings to the gods.

In AD 230, a sweeter version of cheesecake came from the Greek writer Athenaeus: "Take cheese and pound it till smooth and pasty; put cheese in a brazen sieve; add honey and spring wheat flour. Heat in one mass, cool, and serve."

## THE DEVIL'S IN THE DETAILS

Cheesecake plays a role in the musical *Guys and Dolls*, during a pivotal scene where the characters Nathan and Sky meet. In the 1955 movie version, Frank Sinatra plays Nathan, who is eating a piece of cheesecake when Sky, played by Marlon Brando, approaches. Sinatra apparently hated cheesecake, so practical joker Brando made one mistake after another to force Sinatra to redo the scene many times.

The conquering Roman armies took the concept and ran with it, bringing it to every corner of Europe by AD 10000. Versions of cheesecake were brought over to the New World throughout the 18th and 19th centuries. The cheeses used at this time were closer to a farmers' or cottage cheese and involved work to make it creamy and smooth.

This all changed in 1872 in Upstate New York when cream cheese was invented, making the creation of a creamy, smooth cheesecake easier than ever. William Lawrence, a dairyman from Chester, New York, was working on some new cheese formulas, trying to mimic the soft, mild Neufchâtel cheese from France. In the process, he accidently created cream cheese. He sold it in foil, and it became known as Philadelphia cream cheese. In 1912, James Kraft improved on the recipe, pasteurizing it and bringing it to the masses.

No one knows specifically which individual first blended industrialized cream cheese with cheesecake recipes. Cultural tradition, however, credits Jewish immigrants in New York City with masterminding this king of desserts. Bragging rights, however, for best restaurant cheesecake have been claimed by one Arnold Reuben. According to some foodies, Reuben (1883–1970) was a German-born Jewish immigrant who would grow to become a legend in the New York culinary scene in the first half of the 20th century. Whether fact or fiction, Reuben supposedly claimed that he tasted a cream-cheese-based cheesecake at the home of a friend sometime before 1929. After tasting the hearty treat, he immediately began experimenting with the recipe and serving the cake in his popular Turf Restaurant at 49th Street and Broadway in New York City.

## COMMON CHEESE CAKE

from *Directions for Cookery in its Various Branches* by Eliza Leslie (1840)

Boil a quart of rich milk. Beat eight eggs, put them in the milk, and let the milk and eggs boil together till they become a curd. Then drain it through a very clean sieve till all the whey is out. Put the curd into a deep dish and mix with it half a pound of butter, working them well together. When it is cold, add to it the beaten yolks of four eggs, and four large tablespoonfuls of powdered white sugar; also a grated nutmeg. Lastly, stir in by degrees half a pound of currants that have been previously picked, washed, dried, and dredged with flour. Lay puff paste around the rim of the dish, and bake cheesecake half an hour. Send it to table cold.

# FISH STICKS

........................●........................

**I WOULD LIKE TO GO FISHING AND CATCH A FISH STICK, THAT WOULD BE CONVENIENT.**

—Mitch Hedberg

**ARCHAEOLOGICAL EVIDENCE SUGGESTS** humans (and our hominid ancestors) have been eating fish for almost two million years. Freshwater fish were the first major aquatic resource to be plundered, but as technology and civilizations evolved, saltwater fish soon became one of the most vital resources for human existence around the globe. Wars have been fought, economies built and ravaged, and ways of life have all been built on the consumption of fish.

As impressive as all that is, it's hard not to pity those poor souls who had to survive centuries of nonrectangular fish consumption. According to some sources, the fish stick, or fish finger as it's known across the Atlantic, was first invented in the early 1950s in the United Kingdom. Earlier versions of frozen fish may have developed in fishing villages in the United States much earlier, but no material evidence has popped up to support this theory. Still, the practicality of freezing fish at sea and then transporting the preserved product is so obvious that it's likely the idea of frozen fish has existed for much longer than sixty years.

Humans had been battering nd deep-frying fish since the mid-19th century.

However, it wasn't until after World War II that Americans seemed to be ready to embrace pre-prepared fish on a national level.

In 1953, Gorton-Pew Fisheries introduced the frozen fish stick to America, and a new age of human-seafood relations began. By 1955, nine million pounds of frozen precooked fish sticks were sold in America. There are numerous recipes from that time period that describe fish fillets dipped in egg then bread crumbs, and fried.

## THE DEVIL'S IN THE DETAILS

Parents the world over thank Neptune for fish sticks. Most would prefer their children to eat steamed scrod, but when you've got a picky kid and not much time to prepare dinner, at least fish sticks do contain some semblance of a healthy meal. They are easy to make from scratch: Slice a frozen fillet of any white fish into pieces, dip the pieces quickly in beaten egg then in Panko bread crumbs. Cook on parchment paper in a 400°F oven for 15 minutes and serve with ketchup. Tell them it's chicken nuggets if they fuss!

The one included on the next page even suggests cutting the fillets into squares and stacking them in a pyramid. Perhaps Martha Stewart took a page or two from Mrs. Isabella Beeton, author of *The Book of Household Management!*

# } FRIED FILLETED SOLES {

from *The Book of Household Management* by Mrs. Isabella Beeton (1861)

Time: About 10 minutes. Seasonable at any time. Sufficient: 2 large soles for 6 persons. Soles for filleting should be large, as the flesh can be more easily separated from the bones, and there is less waste. Skin and wash the fish, and raise the meat carefully from the bones, and divide it into nice handsome pieces. The more usual way is to roll the fillets, after dividing each one in two pieces, and either bind them round with twine, or run a small skewer through them. Brush over with egg, and cover with bread crumbs; fry them, and garnish with fried parsley and cut lemon. When a pretty dish is desired, this is by far the most elegant mode of dressing soles, as they look much better than when fried whole. Instead of rolling the fillets, they may be cut into square pieces, and arranged in the shape of a pyramid on the dish.

# WAFFLE

HE GAVE HER A LOOK THAT YOU COULD
OF POURED ON A WAFFLE.

—Ring Lardner

**NO SUNDAY MORNING** would be complete without a warm waffle topped with syrup, powdered sugar, and strawberries. The waffle has a long history of happy stomachs, and Americans are pleased to continue the tradition.

The waffle as we know it first appeared in the 13th century with the invention of the cooking plates. A craftsman forged two iron plates that sandwiched the dough between them, creating that characteristic honeycomb pattern. The Old French word for waffle (*wafla*) means "a piece of honeybee hive." Early craftsmen were creative with their waffle iron designs, adding landscapes, coats of arms, or religious symbols instead of the honeycomb. The devices were a set of hinged plates that would press together over the dough. Wooden handles were attached so the dough could be held over a fire to bake, and then be flipped manually.

Vendors selling waffles began popping up all over medieval France and sold waffles at church doors for religious celebrations or saint's days. France's King Charles IX had to regulate the vendors' business when their numbers grew too large and they began to fight among themselves for space. His decree was that there must be a six-foot distance between each vendor.

Throughout the 16th century, waffles were eaten through all echelons of society. The ingredients varied from bad flour for the poor to milk, eggs, and honey for the rich. Waffles were soon on the move. In 1620, Dutch "wafles" landed on American shores with the Pilgrims due to a layover in Holland before continuing on to America.

These batter-based flat cakes gained a new form of popularity in America when Thomas Jefferson returned from his stint in France as a diplomat. In 1789 he presented his friends with a long-handled waffle iron. This machine enclosed the batter and gave a new crispness to the iconic shape.

On August 24, 1869, Cornelius Swarthout of New York patented the first U.S. waffle iron that is heated over a coal stove. The waffle iron goes stove-free in 1911 when General Electric introduces the first electric waffle iron with a built-in thermostat to keep waffles from burning. The basic mechanics developed by Thomas J. Steckbeck are the launching point for today's waffle irons. Waffles continued to grow in popularity, and during the 1930s, waffle irons became standard kitchen appliances. Brothers Tony, Sam, and Frank Dorsa filled the need for instant waffles and introduced frozen toaster waffles called Froffles in 1953. The name was changed once people began

**THE DEVIL'S IN THE DETAILS**

In the 1880s, "waffle frolics" started popping up. During these parties, guests enjoyed either sweet waffles with maple syrup or a savory version topped with kidney stew. In the American South, a meal of waffles with creamed chicken eventually took hold. Anything tasty was thought to be even tastier on a waffle.

calling them Eggos for their "eggy" taste. Kellogg purchased the brand from the brothers during the 1970s.

During the New York World's Fair in 1964, thick Belgian waffles made with yeast and topped with fruit and whipped cream came onto the scene. Maurice Vermersch gained fame for his Belgian waffles, made from his wife's recipe when they were living in Brussels. His recipes were so popular back home he was determined to share them at the world's fair. The Belgian waffle has since made a happy home in the United States.

## MRS. B.'S WAFFLES

from *Miss Beecher's Domestic Receipt Book* by Catherine E. Beecher (1858)

One quart of flour, and a teaspoonful of salt. One qurt of sour milk, with two tablespoonfulls of butter melted in it. Five well-beated eggs. A teaspoonful for more of saleratus [precursor of baking soda], enough to sweeten the milk. Baked in waffle irons. Some like one tea-cup full of sugar added.

# PIZZA

YOU BETTER CUT THE PIZZA IN FOUR PIECES
BECAUSE I'M NOT HUNGRY ENOUGH TO EAT SIX.
—Yogi Berra

**PIZZA IS ARGUABLY** America's favorite food. The proof is in the millions of empty pizza boxes lying scattered about every Friday night. With thousands of years to be perfected, it's no wonder why Americans are so devoted to savoring delicious pizza.

The ancestor of the pizza is thought to have been prepared since the Neolithic Age. Throughout history, people like the ancient Greeks, the bakers of the ancient world, have been adding ingredients to flat bread to make it more flavorful. These early flat breads were sometimes covered with cheese and local ingredients like dates, herbs, or onions and then baked.

Pizza was born as a peasant dish when the poor in Naples, Italy, began adding tomatoes to their yeast-based flat breads. The first pizzerias followed suit, beginning as small open-air stands. Many credit Antica Pizzeria Port'Alba as being the city's first pizzeria, which is still serving pizza to this day. Neapolitans are serious about their pizza and believe there are only two true archetypal pizzas—marinara and Margherita. Marinara came first, topped with tomato, garlic, oregano, and extra virgin olive oil. Raffaele Espositio is widely credited for creating the Margherita pizza in 1889. Topped with tomato sauce, mozzarella cheese, and fresh basil, the pizza was made to evoke the colors of the Italian flag in honor of Queen Margherita of Savoy.

It's still a mystery as to how pizza got its name. John Mariani speculates in his *Dictionary of Italian Food and Drink* that the term may derive from an old Italian word, *pizzicare*, meaning to "pinch" or "pluck". This may refer to the way in which something is plucked quickly from an oven. Men who worked at pizzerias were in turn called *pizzaioli*, and by the 19th century, the word *pizza* referred to the pies themselves.

## THE DEVIL'S IN THE DETAILS

Pepperoni is American's favorite topping, with more than 250 million pounds consumed on pizzas every year in the United States. Although there is no exact record of the first time pepperoni was used on a pizza, it became popular between 1930 and 1950. Americans eat an average of forty-six slices of pizza a year, from the three billion pizzas sold each year in the United States.

Pizza first traveled to the United State at the end of the 19th century with immigrants from Southern Italy. Pizza was soon sold in Italian neighborhoods within major cities across America. Over time, a few distinctive forms of American pizza began to appear. The East Coast adopted a thin-crust style of pizza, also known as New York style. Gennaro Lombardi is credited with selling some of the first slices out of his place at 53rd ½ Spring Street in Little Italy around 1905. Ike Sewell and Ric Riccardo are credited with inventing Chicago's deep-dish style of pizza at Pizzeria Uno around 1943. Meanwhile, the West Coast opted for more gourmet pizzas with vibrant toppings and a thicker crust.

Pizza's popularity exploded after World War II, and soon it was no longer just Italian immigrants dining at pizzerias. Allied troops stationed in Italy took their appreciation for the dish back home, and soon, the modern pizza industry was born. Chain restaurants quickly began popping up all over America; the first Pizza Hut sprang up in Wichita, Kansas, around 1958. It was also during the 1950s that the first frozen pizzas began lining the shelves at grocery stores. One of the earliest print references is Jo Bucci's "Method for Making Frozen Pizza," filed in Philadelphia, Pennsylvania, in 1950. Today, companies that specialize in pizza delivery dominate the American pizza business. Why dine out when you can have your piping-hot pizza at home?

While the basic recipe for pizza has never gone out of style, there are still plenty of appetizing experiments being done with the dish. Today, you can order a classic Margherita or branch out and explore the uncharted realm of the deep-dish pizza. There is no wrong way to enjoy a slice of pizza.

# HOT DOG

......................•......................

"I WOULD LIKE TO BUY ONE OF YOUR HOT DOGS . . . MAY I
SELECT MY OWN?" IGNATIUS ASKED, PEERING DOWN OVER
THE TOP OF THE POT. "I SHALL PRETEND THAT I AM IN A
SMART RESTAURANT AND THAT THIS IS THE LOBSTER POND."

— John Kennedy Toole, *A Confederacy of Dunces*

**WHETHER IT'S SLATHERED** in relish and ketchup, covered in chili and cheese, or just served naked on a bun, the hot dog is, at its core, a sausage. And those have been around since 850 BC, mentioned in none other than Homer's *Odyssey*. In AD 64, a sausage was made for Emperor Nero Claudius Caesar by his cook, Gaius. Apparently, a pig's intestines popped out on cleaning a whole roasted pig and Gaius had a eureka moment. He filled the intestines with ground meat.

Jump to the 1690s, and you start hearing about sausages made in Germany, the sausage capital of the world. Another popular theory suggests that hot dogs were first created in Coburg, Germany, by a butcher named Johann Georghehner sometime in the late 1600s. Not to be outdone, the city of Frankfurt, Germany, also lays claim to the hot dog. (In 1987, the city celebrated the five hundredth anniversary of the hot dog.)

Naturally, German and Eastern European immigrants brought with them their recipes, and by mid-19th century, the hot dog had firmly arrived in the United States. Not surprisingly, the hot dog immediately took off in East Coast cities as a favored urban snack food. The portable treat quickly became associated with quick lunches, leisure events, and early American sports.

**THE DEVIL'S IN THE DETAILS**

Baseball fans devoured 27.5 million hot dogs at major-league parks this year, according to The National Hot Dog and Sausage Council.

By 1871, Charles Feltman opened one of the first hot dog stands in Coney Island, New York. One of his employees, Nathan Handwerker, a Polish immigrant, started Nathan's in 1916 with another small hot dog stand in Coney Island. His hot dogs were cheaper. It was his wife's recipe that really made Nathan's stand out. The popularity of the hot dog helped spur numerous local butchers into national chains in the early 20th century. In 1939, Papaya King open, spurring other hot dog franchises to move in.

Numerous theories exist as to why a nonspicy German sausage earned the name "hot dog," the most obvious of which is the sausage's resemblance to dachshund breed of dogs. The most popular theory, however, states that the phrase "hot dog" was coined by an American cartoonist in New York sometime around 1901. Tad Dorgan was supposedly observing the games at New York's Polo Grounds on a cold April day when he saw numerous street vendors selling "red hot" dachshund dogs to fans. Dorgan wanted to capture the moment, but in the age before spell-check, he had no idea how to spell "dachshund." Instead, Dorgan wrote a caption with street sellers trying to hawk "hot dogs." No one has managed to locate this cartoon, but the theory has yet to be completely disproven. Still other sources claim the phrase "hot dog" had to be coined much earlier. Historians point to numerous college magazines from the late 1890s that use the phrase "dog wagon" and "hot dog" to describe the late-night edible antics of some students.

## THE DEVIL'S IN THE DETAILS

Hot dogs are served across America, but many cities have their own distinct toppings, such as:

*New York City: Mustard and sauerkraut on a steamed bun

*Boston: Mustard and relish on a New England-style bun

*Chicago: Yellow mustard on the dog, with diced tomatoes, dill pickle or sweet relish, pickled peppers, and celery salt

*Kansas City: Sauerkraut and Swiss cheese

*Cincinnati: Cincinnati chili, cheddar cheese, diced onions, and Ohio's own Bertman Ballpark mustard

*Detroit: Beanless chili, diced onion, and yellow mustard

*Los Angeles: Bacon-wrapped, grilled onions, jalapeños, bell peppers, mustard, ketchup and salsa

*Seattle: Cream cheese and grilled onions

# MAPLE SYRUP

"IS THERE SUGAR IN SYRUP?
—Will Ferrell in *Elf*

**TO PANCAKE LOVERS**, it's worth its weight in gold. Maple syrup is one of those traditional American treats that have been almost universally popular since the moment they were first consumed.

Maple syrup is truly a native foodstuff of America. According to oral traditions, supported by archeological evidence, the Native Americans living in the north tapped maple trees for their sap, which they called "sweet water," *Sinzibuckwud* (literally "drawn from trees"). The bright winter daylight that occurs throughout January and February triggers sugar maples (*Acer saccharum*) to expel a sweet clear liquid. When cooked over a high flame, the sugars in this liquid distill into a thicker, sweeter syrup—but experimenters be warned, it takes a lot of liquid to make a descent amount of syrup.

American colonists supposedly learned how to collect this liquid sometime in the early 1600s. According to the New England Maple

Museum, the first European to supposedly learn this technique was a French missionary sometime around 1690.

Sweeteners were expensive for colonists, and maple by-products quickly became incorporated into early American cooking. It was neither quick nor simple, but it was free.

## THE DEVIL'S IN THE DETAILS

Maple syrup comes in a number of different variations. The United States Department of Agriculture grades it with five different grades. From lightest to darkest in color (which winds up corresponding pretty closely to taste, and the darker the syrup, the stronger the flavor): Grade A light amber, grade A medium amber, grade A dark amber, grade B maple syrup, and commercial grade. All are delicious, with far more taste than the caramel-colored corn syrup that many Americans accept on their morning pancakes.

# { A RECIPE TO MAKE MAPLE SUGAR }

from *The Frugal Housewife* by Susannah Carter (1803)

Make an incision in a number of maple trees, at the same time, about the middle of February, and receive the juice of them in wooden or earthen vessels. Strain this juice (after it is drawn from the sediment) and boil it in a wide mouthed kettle. Place the kettle directly over the fire, in such a manner that the flame shall not play upon its sides. Skim the liquor when it is boiling. When it is reduced to a thick syrup and cooled, strain it again, and let it settle for two or three days, in which time it will be fit for granulating. This operation is performed by filling the kettle half full of syrup, and boiling it a second time. To prevent its boiling over, add to it a piece of fresh butter or fat of the size of a walnut. You may easily determine when it is sufficiently boiled to granulate, by cooling a little of it. It must then be put into bags or baskets through which the water will drain. The sugar, if refined by the usual process, may be made into as good single or double refined loaves, as were ever made from the sugar obtained from the juice of the West Indian cane.

# COTTON CANDY

### CANDY IS DANDY BUT LIQUOR IS QUICKER.

—Ogden Nash

**SINCE THE** Saint Louis World's Fair of 1904, Americans have been fascinated by cotton candy. The fluffy pink stuff, originally called fairy floss, is a common sight at fairs, baseball games, and circuses. However, this summertime airy treat has been creating sticky fingers for longer than most would imagine.

At its base, cotton candy is no more than spun sugar. As far back as the 1400s, Italians delighted in making spun sugar desserts by hand. The method was laborious and involved melting the sugar and then using a fork to make strings of sugar over an upside-down bowl. After the sugar dried, they were able to gather the fibers and serve them as dessert. Even up through the 18th century, European confectioners made spun sugar webs painted in gold and sugar nests for Easter eggs. The skill required made this primitive cotton candy too expensive for the masses.

Nashville candy makers John C. Wharton and William Morrison are believed to have patented the first electric cotton candy machine in 1897. The machine was perfect for collecting the delicate cottony strands onto paper sticks or into bags. It worked by utilizing centrifugal force to spin and melt the sugar through holes in a screen, where the fibers could be collected on the other side. The two candy makers put their invention to the test during the Saint Louis World's Fair and were greeted with throngs of curious fairgoers. The machine was soon produced in mass quantities because it was portable, the process was novel, and the appeal was widespread. Cotton candy became the perfect fair food.

**THE DEVIL'S IN THE DETAILS**

No one quite knows why it's in winter since we usually have cotton candy at summer fairs, or who started it or, really, what rituals are practiced during it, but National Cotton Candy Day is celebrated on December 7.

It is argued, however, that Thomas Patton was the first to create the cotton candy machine, and he did receive a patent for his gas-powered model. And in 1900, Patton is credited with creating a love match between the Ringling Brothers Circus and cotton candy. A day at the circus was now just a little bit sweeter.

Ironically, dentist Josef Delarose Lascaux is another contender for inventor of cotton candy. He never received a patent for his machine but was said to have given cotton candy out to his patients at his Louisiana dental office. That's one way to keep business going.

During the 1920s, cotton candy became the universal name for candy floss. The sugary treat continued to grow in popularity, and in the 1970s, the cotton candy machine became an automated giant that could bag the candy on a massive scale. Cotton candy is no longer just a fair food; it can be bought at the grocery store, or even made at home on a personal cotton candy machine.

## SPINNING SUGAR

from *Desserts and Salads by Gesine Lemcke* (1920)

Put 3/4 pound loaf sugar in a small copper kettle, add sufficient cold water to half cover the sugar and stir until it is melted; then place the kettle over a strong fire and boil the sugar to a crack (the 6th grade); add a few drops vinegar, remove the kettle, dip it for a few minutes into cold water and let it cool off a little; if the sugar is spun when too hot the threads will be too thin and lumps will form; then place the kettle in a pan of hot water, or on the side of stove, to keep the sugar warm; take a large knife in the left hand and hold it out straight before you; take a silver spoon in the right hand, dip it into the sugar without touching the bottom of kettle and let some of the sugar run off from the spoon; then spin long threads back and forth over the knife from right to left; after a considerable amount of sugar is spun in this way take it from the knife, lay on clean paper and spin the rest in like manner; when all is spun form the sugar into pompoms, garlands, bouquets, etc.

Half the sugar may be colored with cochineal to a delicate pink. The sugar should be spun in a place free from draughts and in clear and dry weather. This sugar is used for decorating and trimming dishes.

# TWINKIE

•

"YOU GET A BIG DELIGHT IN EVERY BITE OF HOSTESS
TWINKLE CAKES"

—Advertisement

**LIKE IT OR NOT**, the Twinkie has become a part of American food history.

It was first invented in 1930 by James A. Dewar of Schiller Park, Illinois. Dewar was working for Continental Baking Company at the time and had been looking for way to sell shortbread cakes year-round. The traditional sponge cake was usually served with strawberries, which made the snack a summer specialty. Dewar chose to fill small pan-baked cakes with banana filling as a substitute for strawberries. During World War II, a shortage of bananas prompted the company to fill Twinkies with vanilla filling instead. The new and improved Twinkie remains the best-selling Hostess food product to this day.

It was only a matter of time before the Twinkie was deep-fried. This phenomenon has swept state fairs and carnivals nationwide.

# BUBBLE GUM

I FELT PRETTY GOOD WHILE I WAS BLOWING THAT BUBBLE, BUT AS SOON AS THE GUM LOST ITS FLAVOR, I WAS BACK TO PONDERING MY MORTALITY.

—Mitch Hedberg

**GUM ISN'T ALLOWED** in school—which might be why Americans tend to pop their first piece at a very tender age. They come from it honestly. Archaeologists have determined that the very wise ancient Greeks were among the first Europeans to chew recreationally. A resin produced from a small shrub that grows along the Mediterranean, called *mastiche*, was the ancient version of Juicy Fruit. The resin was collected, boiled, and then chewed by the Greeks. Recent discoveries Northern European bogs also point to the harvesting of *mastiche* and more resin chewing in Germany and Scandinavia as early as the Middle Stone Age.

Across the Atlantic, ancient Mayans chewed sap from sapodilla trees while North American tribes did the same with the sap from spruce trees. Americans retained a strong interest in chewing, and by 1848, John B. Curtis marketed the first commercial chewing gum in Maine. State of Maine Pure Spruce Gum was quickly followed by other flavored gums.

On December 28, 1869, William F. Semple of Mount Vernon, Ohio, received the first U.S. patent for "a new and improved Chewing-Gum." Semple wanted to include rubber with this new chewing gum, but he made sure to note this would be a nonvulcanized compound.

The true turning point in the evolution of chewing gum came in 1888 when the Thomas Adams Gum Company introduced the first vending machine to sell gum in a New York City subway

THE DEVIL'S IN THE DETAILS

Bubble gum went global during World War II, when American soldiers chewed the tasty treat while fighting abroad. Before sugar shortages halted gum manufacturing, bubble gum was even included as an accessory ration for American troops.

station. Both the Tutti-Frutti flavor and the machine itself were a hit. Other rival companies popped up shortly thereafter. In Chicago, William Wrigley Jr. began manufacturing gum in 1892. The Lotta and Vassar flavors are lost to history, but with the introduction of Juicy Fruit and Spearmint in 1893, Wrigley changed the world of mastication. In 1899, Franklin V. Canning created the Dentyne gum brand in New York.

The idea for a "bubble" gum first appeared in 1906 under the brand name "Blibber-Blubber." Unfortunately for gum lovers, Blibber never made it to the market.

Chewers across America had to wait until 1928 for the first bubble gum to be sold in stores. It was an accident! Walter Diemer, who was an accountant at the Fleer Chewing Gum Company in Philadelphia, had been fooling around with chewing gum recipes in his spare time when a batch seemed oddly stretchy and less sticky than others. The formula was a hit, becoming Double Bubble bubble gum.

Diemer, who was twenty-three years old at the time, never received royalties for his creation. He said he didn't care, and he remained at Fleer until 1985.

According to the British newspaper the *Guardian*, "After his first wife died in 1990, Diemer rode a big tricycle around his Pennsylvania retirement village and gave bubble gum to children."